WAITING FOR GODOT

CONTINUUM CHARACTER STUDIES

WAITING FOR GODOT
CHARACTER STUDIES

PAUL LAWLEY

continuum

Continuum
The Tower Building
11 York Road
London SE1 7NX

80 Maiden Lane, Suite 704
New York
NY 10038

www.continuumbooks.com

© Paul Lawley 2008

First published 2008

British Library Cataloguing-in-Publication Data
A catalogue record for this book is available from the British Library.

ISBN: 978-08264-9380-4 (hardback)
978-08264-9381-1 (paperback)

Library of Congress Cataloging-in-Publication Data
A catalog record for this book is available from the Library of Congress.

Typeset by Servis Filmsetting Ltd, Manchester
Printed and bound in Great Britain by
MPG Books Ltd, Bodmin, Cornwall

This book is dedicated to my mother, and
to the memory of my father.

CONTENTS

SERIES EDITOR'S PREFACE

This series aims to promote sophisticated literary analysis through the concept of character. It demonstrates the necessity of linking character analysis to texts' themes, issues and ideas, and encourages students to embrace the complexity of literary characters and the texts in which they appear. The series thus fosters close critical reading and evidence-based discussion, as well as an engagement with historical context, and with literary criticism and theory.

Character Studies was prompted by a general concern in literature departments about students responding to literary characters as if they were real people rather than fictional creations, and writing about them as if they were two-dimensional entities existing in an ahistorical space. Some students tend to think it is enough to observe that King Lear goes 'mad', that Frankenstein is 'ambitious', or that Vladimir and Estragon are 'tender and cruel'. Their comments are correct, but obviously limited.

Thomas Docherty, in his *Reading (Absent) Character: Towards a Theory of Characterization in Fiction*, reminds us to relate characters to ideas but also stresses the necessity of engaging with the complexity of characters:

> If we proceed with the same theory as we apply to allegory [that a character represents one thing, such as Obstinate in Bunyan's *Pilgrim's Progress*], then we will be led to accept that Madame Bovary 'means' or 'represents' some one essence or value, however complex that essence may be. But perhaps, and more likely, she is many things, and perhaps some of them

lead to her character being incoherent, lacking unity, and so on. [. . .] It is clearly wrong to say, in a critical reading, that Kurtz, for example, in Conrad's *Heart of Darkness* represents evil, or ambition, or any other one thing, and to leave it at that; nor is Jude a representative of 'failed aspirations' in Hardy's *Jude the Obscure*; nor is Heathcliff a representation of the proletariat in Emily Brontë's *Wuthering Heights*, and so on. There may be elements of truth in some of these readings of character, but the theory which rests content with trying to discover the singular simple essence of character in this way is inadequate [. . .] (1983, p. xii)

King Lear, for example, is complex, so not easily understandable, and is perhaps 'incoherent, lacking unity'; he is fictional, so must be treated as a construct; and he does not 'mean' or 'represent' one thing. We can relate him to ideas about power, control, judgement, value, sovereignty, the public and the private, sex and sexuality, the body, nature and nurture, appearance, inheritance, socialization, patriarchy, religion, will, blindness, sanity, violence, pessimism, hope, ageing, love, death, grief – and so on.

To ignore this, and to respond to Lear as if he is a real person talking ahistorically, means we simplify both the character and the play; it means, in short, that we forget our responsibilities as literary critics. When, for example, Lear cries, 'Howl, howl, howl, howl! O, you are men of stones!' (V.ii.255), it would be wrong to ignore our emotional response, to marginalize our empathy for a father carrying his dead daughter, but we must also engage with such other elements as: the meaning and repetition of 'Howl' (three howls in some editions, four in others); the uncertainty about to whom 'you are men of stones' is directed; what 'men of stones' meant to Shakespeare's audience; the various ways in which the line can be said, and the various effects produced; how what Lear says relates to certain issues in the play and introduces new ideas about being human; what literary critics have written about the line; and what literary theorists have said, or might say, about it.

When we embrace the complexity of character, when we undertake detailed, sensitive critical analysis that acknowledges historical context, and literary criticism and theory, and when we relate characters to themes, issues and ideas, the texts we study blossom, beautifully and wonderfully, and we realize that we have so much more to say about them. We are also reminded of why they are worthy of study, of why they are important, of why they are great.

Ashley Chantler
University of Chester, UK

ACKNOWLEDGEMENTS

I am grateful to Faber and Faber Ltd (UK and British Commonwealth) and Grove/Atlantic, Inc. (USA) for permission to quote from the plays of Samuel Beckett.

I should like to thank my friends Nick Smart (for initial advice and encouragement) and Terry Enright (for discussions about theatre over the years). To Vincent Mahon, who read and commented on the manuscript, I owe a continuing intellectual debt as enduring as his own gift of friendship. Discussions with the late James Hansford leave their traces in whatever I write. For careful scrutiny of the manuscript, my thanks go to Mary Jacobs and Barbara Oprics. Valuable questions and suggestions came from Vahid Norouzalibeik in Tehran, who has translated *Godot* into Farsi. My thanks go to Philip Jones for his interest and usual generosity. Above all, I am happy to record my debt to Angela Moorjani, whose friendship, encouragement and example have energized me throughout. Her reading of the manuscript was intellectually bracing and endlessly stimulating. Frances Waters and Ben were with me as I wrote: my love and gratitude to them, as ever. Any errors and omissions are of course my own.

INTRODUCTION: AN OVERVIEW OF *WAITING FOR GODOT*

WHAT HAPPENS IN *WAITING FOR GODOT?*

Here is one answer to that question.

Two old men, companions for more than 50 years, wait on a country road for a Mr Godot (pronounced GOD-oh). While waiting they speculate about the mysterious Godot, contemplate suicide and attempt to tell a joke. One concerns himself with his boot, sleeps and eats a carrot; the other revolves a biblical conundrum and endures a bladder condition. Their solitude is relieved when a local landowner comes by, accompanied by the carrier he is hoping to sell at the market. He has the carrier tethered on the end of a rope. Neither of these is Mr Godot. The landowner settles down to a brief picnic and a smoke. One of the old men is outraged by his treatment of his carrier; the other begs his left-over bones. The landowner warms to the men and responds expansively to their questions. He generously explains the twi-light to them. When sympathetically approached, the carrier kicks one of the men; but when the landowner feels entertain-ment should be provided, it is the carrier who is required to dance, then to think out loud for the delectation of the others. When the Think spirals out of control, the carrier is restrained. Landowner and carrier depart after ceremonious farewells, leaving the old men alone together again. Soon afterwards, however, a boy enters bringing a message from Mr Godot, who, he reports, cannot come today but will come tomorrow. One of the men questions the boy, with little success, and when the boy leaves, night falls immediately. The other old man recalls a suicide attempt, and they consider parting. They resolve to go, but stay where they are.

The two old men are called Vladimir (nicknamed Didi) and Estragon (French for the herb tarragon; nicknamed Gogo). The landowner is called Pozzo (Italian for 'well'; pronounced Pot'so) and his carrier Lucky. 'All four wear bowlers' (p. 33), says a tardy footnote, thus disclosing the single most famous fact about the look of the characters as if it were an absentminded after-thought.

In the second of two Acts, the tripartite pattern is repeated: Before-With-After. It is the same place and (an authorial direction informs us) the next day. Bafflingly, the solitary tree that was bare yesterday now has three leaves. Vladimir sings a song, tries to convince Estragon that they are happy and prompts him to remember what happened yesterday. Estragon tries on the boots which he had left there yesterday, refuses a radish and sleeps. Finding Lucky's hat, they make a game of swapping hats; they play at being Pozzo and Lucky, and even at being the tree; they play at insulting each other, and at reconciliation. They get frightened and stand on watch. When Pozzo and Lucky enter again, the rope is now shorter, and Lucky leads his master. The pair immediately falls. Vladimir and Estragon debate at length what to do next in response to Pozzo's pleas for assistance, but when they try to help, they both fall down themselves. They rise, and raise Pozzo, who reveals that he is now blind and Lucky dumb. Estragon tries to take revenge on the fallen Lucky for the Act I kick, but when this attempt comes to grief he falls asleep. Pozzo rebuffs Vladimir's questions furiously, and then is led off by Lucky, whose bags are now, the master says, filled with sand. Speculating that Pozzo was only pretending to be blind, Vladimir tries to discuss the visitors with Estragon, but the latter falls asleep again after struggling with his boot. In a monologue Vladimir takes stock of their situation. The Boy enters, and Vladimir anticipates that he has the same message as yesterday from Mr Godot. He leaves; night falls. The old men again contemplate suicide, and again consider parting. They again resolve to go, but again stay where they are.

Another response to the question of what happens might be: 'it depends what you mean by "happen"'. When Vivian Mercier famously described *Waiting for Godot* as 'a play in which nothing happens, twice' (qtd in Boxall 2000, p. 13), he was heading off this 'philosophical' response by introducing a pleasant conundrum about Nothing. In his statement the vacancy of nothing takes on the substance of a grammatical subject: Nothing *can* happen, just as something can happen. And in this play, it does. Just as some music can persuade us to listen to silence, and some sculpture invite us to rethink vacant space, so *Godot* enables us to sense emptiness – pressing in ominously behind all the words and all the gestures. As Estragon remarks, 'There's no lack of void' (p. 66), and they are engaged in guarding against its encroachment.

Still, *happening* in this play does call for some consideration, if only for practical reasons. My summary of the play includes some details, but excludes a great many more. How did I know to include these rather than the others? After all, there is no story, to which some details contribute rather than others, so the criterion of narrative sense-making doesn't apply. Might I not have made my brief summary even briefer, as other guides usually do? Two men wait for a Mr Godot on a country road; two other men, a master and his servant, pass by and stop for a while. And so on. Why indeed does Beckett put in the detail he does? Could we cut with impunity? Why did he put in so much? Come to that, why did he not put in more? And why should he have stopped when he did?

These are questions about the structure of the play. But they are not only that. A critic might demonstrate the internal cohesion of the play, showing how one detail echoes another, how one gesture mirrors another, how each part relates non-narratively to every other part; how, that is, the imaginative matrix of the play is fully open to scrutiny – rather like music. Good critics have done this. But this still should not prevent a persisting sense of the *arbitrariness* of it all. To put it another way: the question of why it is not shorter than it is, and the question of why it is not longer than it is, are questions that can be asked of any fiction in any medium. But almost all fictions work to prevent our asking these questions: it may even be said that their success is measured by their ability to prevent us asking these questions. *Waiting for Godot* positively invites us to ask them by consistently highlighting its own artificiality:

> VLADIMIR: This is becoming really insignificant.
> ESTRAGON: Not enough.
>
> (p. 68)

A play is an imitation of an action: the first literary critic (Aristotle) tells us this on the first page of the first surviving critical text (his *Poetics*). The word 'drama' derives from the Greek for a 'thing done'. Drama, then, is the medium of action. But here, in the realm of significant activity, a play gives us the essential passivity of waiting, and nothing else. Then it keeps on reminding us that it is doing this. If the play were not so effectively charged with feeling, we might very well suppose it to be the result of a technical exercise that the playwright had set himself – one of the most difficult imaginable. Indeed there are worse ways of regarding it. Among other things it *is* an extraordinary technical achievement: a paradoxical playing out of inaction in the medium of action, and with a near-minimum of given means. A tree, a stone, hats, boots, vegetables, a piece of rope. It is no wonder that when Pozzo arrives, his shameless brandishing of *things* – his whip, his pipe, his watch, his stool, his chicken – is funny in itself. In this poverty-stricken context, these possessions of Pozzo are above all resources for performance, and he certainly makes the best of them for that purpose. They remind us yet again that the playwright has not just invented, in Vladimir and Estragon, two impoverished characters, but has elected to impoverish himself – to divest himself of as many dramatic means as possible – in the composition of his play.

THE ORIGINALITY OF *GODOT*

Stasis in the theatre was not entirely new. However, to make a whole play out of it, as more than an elaborate joke – this certainly was. Of course drama since the Greeks had always had its moments of inertia, its waitings, its anticipations, its standstills,

4

its deadlocks, its listenings – often memorable ones. But these were resolved by and into action, and therefore understood as phases – *stases* – within a larger action. For more than three long Acts Hamlet, by his own admission, does nothing. Nonetheless, we know that the resolution, the action of revenge, will come. The hero has 'that within which passeth show' (*Hamlet* I.ii.85), and in response to it, the interest plunges inwards, the focus becomes psychological and the dynamics of inner conflict drive the action to its outcome. Not surprisingly, then, when at the turn of the twentieth century dramatists become newly interested in stasis as an inescapable condition of spiritual or social existence, the shift is again inwards. In the symbolist plays of the Belgian Maurice Maeterlinck (*The Blind* (1890) is an example), a mysterious soulscape is evoked through verbal and visual suggestion, effecting a sense of spiritual disorientation, ignorance or deluded knowledge, which is shared by characters who are often barely distinguishable from one another. And in the plays of Anton Chekhov, such as *The Cherry Orchard* (1904), the increasing social and historical dislocation of the Russian aristocracy, and of Russian society generally, is implied by a potentially disruptive emotional subtext stirring underneath a placid, inactive, even trivial social surface. The action – what is really happening – is catastrophic, but its epicentre is always, almost by definition, else-where, invisible and scarcely audible. The artist gauges its rever-berations, resonances and aftershocks. Little or nothing happens, yet somehow everything is different. For these playwrights, stasis has become a condition of being, in a world grown strange and growing stranger.

Neither Maeterlinck nor Chekhov can be considered an influence on Beckett. His dialogue, with its emphasis on quasi-musical pattern and rhythm rather than character, can some-times resemble Maeterlinck's, and his tone, with its quirky tragicomic ambiguity, can recall Chekhov's. But he derives nothing directly from either writer, even if impressions were deeply absorbed. (He spoke warmly of Chekhov.) They are perhaps best regarded as his precursors in divining the need for a drama which addressed the question of *stasis* in the medium of *action*. This need was, for each of them, as it was to be for

Beckett, a matter of expressive importance, and not just a technical puzzle. In fact we should do well to recognize that this is one of those instances where technical problem meets expressive need – and meets it head on. In cases like this, we should acknowledge that technique is, as Ezra Pound believed it was, 'the test of a man's sincerity' (1960, p. 9).

Waiting for Godot, then, owes no specific debt to the dramatic tradition in respect of situation. As far as its elements are concerned, however, it is clearly and unashamedly indebted to a number of sources. The chief of these was immediately identified when the play first appeared: the comic 'cross-talk' which was still familiar in the 1950s – if only because fresh in memory – from the music hall or the vaudeville. Moments of slapstick physical action (the falls, the hat-exchange, the boot-business, the kick, the dropping trousers) fall into a slightly different but closely related category, being more specifically clownish and therefore pointing us towards the circus. A taste for clowns had been apparent in French art and writing since the late nineteenth century, and clowns were certainly fashionable among intellectuals in France in the 1920s and 1930s. So when the playwright Jean Anouilh, commenting on the first production, famously described *Godot* as 'The music-hall sketch of Pascal's *Pensées* as played by the Fratellini clowns' (Graver and Federman 1979, p. 92), he was in no danger of being misunderstood by his readers. This was no slur on intellectual dignity: in post-war Paris metaphysics and farce were recognizable bedfellows. Indeed the clown could bring the tragic note with him. Describing the Fratellini (three clown-brothers who parodied the social hierarchy in their physical comedy), J. B. Priestley remarked, 'it was very funny and yet rather sad at the same time. Great clowns are able to mix our feelings in this way' (1975, p. 166).

The more precise points of reference are filmic (though most of the silent-screen comedians in fact had their origins in the halls): Charlie Chaplin (called Charlot in France) for silent slapstick and the comic tramp figure; Buster Keaton (later to appear in Beckett's *Film*) for the fixed disconsolate mask; Stan Laurel and Oliver Hardy for the down-at-heel double act with the characteristic cross-talk of comic and straight-man. All of them made a large number of extremely successful films in the era of silent movies (up to 1930) and beyond, and Beckett was familiar with their work. (The wartime novel *Watt* has a reference to 'a hardy laurel' (Beckett, 1963, p. 253).) Furthermore, in his years as a student in Dublin he had been an enthusiastic theatre-goer, often frequenting venues that, in the words of James Knowlson, 'put him in touch with a lighter kind of theatre that grew out of the revues and music-hall sketches of the "illegitimate" theatre or the circus' (1996, p. 57).

Waiting for Godot thus draws freely on forms of popular theatre. The play certainly answers to the common observation that modern drama is distinguished by its mixture of tones, that in the early twentieth century tragedy becomes grotesque and comedy dark, and that the traditional genres are thus confused and problematized. Not for nothing is it subtitled 'a tragicomedy'. (*En attendant Godot* is not thus subtitled.) However, it does not achieve this through any self-conscious relation to, or influence from, other 'literary' plays, either modern or pre-modern. To his authorized biographer, James Knowlson, Beckett indicated the importance of his fellow Dublin Protestant playwright, John Millington Synge (1871–1909), yet Knowlson is understandably careful to avoid any confident assertion of influence, instead drawing attention to 'atmospheric' characteristics: the resemblance of Vladimir and Estragon to Synge's tramps and beggars; the Irish 'flavour' of their language and turn of their thought; the spareness and poverty of setting. On the level of style and form it is hard to feel that the resemblances are significant ones. What is clear is that the play is energized by popular forms and styles of performance that are hardly at all literary in any important sense.

None of this, of course, is to deny the daunting range of philosophical reference which is implicit in *Godot*. Intellectual culture is there with a vengeance, and not only in the teeming parody of Lucky's Think. It is so deeply absorbed that it rarely shows itself on the surface of the dialogue – which is why speculation about intellectual influences on Beckett's work can be especially frustrating. In fact, the moments when high culture (as distinct from popular) is an identifiable influence are manifest not so much in the words as in the stage-images. 'Painting', writes

Knowlson, 'was in my own view far more important than the theatre of others as a formative influence on [Beckett's] drama' (1992, p. 20).

If anything, the search for influence from painting, notwith-standing our increasing awareness of Beckett's artistic knowl-edge and enthusiasms, is more tenuous than in the case of drama. Nevertheless there can be a degree of certainty. To a scholar-friend, Beckett described a painting by the German artist Caspar David Friedrich (1774–1840) as 'the source of *Waiting for Godot*' (qtd in Knowlson 1996, p. 378). The painting exists in two ver-sions, but *Two Men Contemplating the Moon* (1819), now in Dresden, is the most obvious point of reference. Two men, the younger with his arm round the older, stand with their backs to us in a rugged landscape, observing the moon and the evening star, which are both held within the curve of a gnarled and leafless toppled tree. It is the prototype (if that is the word) for the moonlit endings of each act – especially the first, where Estragon '*contemplates the moon*' and quotes from (or adapts) a poem by an English contemporary of the painter: 'Pale for weariness [. . .] Of climbing heaven and gazing on the likes of us' (p. 52). In addition, Knowlson (Haynes and Knowlson 2003, pp. 73–4) has identified two paintings by Pieter Brueghel the Elder (c. 1525–69) as probable sources for stage images. (As with the Friedrich, Beckett himself as director made visual allusion to them in his productions, but we can speculate that they were present to his visual imagination even as he wrote the text.) These are *The Parable of the Blind* (for Lucky leading Pozzo in Act II) and *The Land of Cockaigne* (for the scene in Act II where all four are on their backs on the ground, pp. 82–4).

So deeply absorbed and so thoroughly 'processed' are the play's influences that even when the author's interests are well documented, we very soon reach the border beyond which all is speculation. It is important, though, not to lose sight of the dis-tinction between the elements out of which the play was made – the most significant of which I have just identified – and the vital dynamic of the play, that is, the reason why it exists in the first place, insofar as that is ascertainable. The most tantalizing of the play's elements – tantalizing because we can never be sure about the extent to which it also forms a part of the vital dynamic – is religion. This I shall consider in my next chapter. But at this point in our investigation we can best gain a perception of the play's motive force by considering the place of *Godot* within its author's writing life.

SHAPING UP TO *GODOT*

'It is the shape that matters', said Samuel Beckett in 1956 (qtd in States 1978, p. viii). He was talking about ideas in general, and one idea in particular, but the same is true of his own life as a writer. To notice the shape he himself gave in retrospect to his own life is a necessary step forward in the understanding of *Waiting for Godot*.

It is well known that Beckett, though willing to answer enquiries limited to fact and matters of information, was extremely reluctant to talk about his own life in any public forum. Indeed his reticence concerning himself and his work attained a virtually mythical status, and with justification. But later in his life he spoke freely, and for the record, with trusted individuals, and seems to have been happy to do so. Expositions of the meanings of texts there were none – not even for actors he was directing or directors he was advising. However he did repeatedly refer to a 'vision', a revelation or turning-point which he experienced and which, to his mind, determined the course of his writing from 1945 onwards. What was the course of the life that was thus 'turned'?

Born in 1906 (on Good Friday, 13 April) into a prosperous Protestant family residing in Foxrock, County Dublin, Beckett as a young man showed an obvious aptitude for study (though certainly not to the exclusion of sport). He studied French and Italian at Trinity College, Dublin, and, after graduation, began a career teaching and lecturing – a career to which it soon became clear he was unsuited. But while working (in 1928–29) as a *lecteur* in English at the Ecole Normale Supérieure in Paris he met his fellow Irishman, the expatriate novelist James Joyce (1882–1941), author of *Dubliners*, *A Portrait of the Artist as a Young Man* and *Ulysses*, and working at that time on what was to become *Finnegans Wake*. Beckett's friendly association with Joyce was vital in his conception of himself as a writer – as indeed it was to his conception of art generally – though in ways which turned out to be far from simple. As Beckett's earliest writing (up to the mid-1930s) shows, the figure of Joyce cast a massive shadow over the young man's imaginative effort even as it enabled him.

After the death of his father in June 1933, Beckett lost his way. These were 'bad years' (Knowlson and Knowlson 2006, p. 67) for him, marked by guilt and depression. Yet this was also valuable experience for his later writing to feed off. He moved from Dublin to London in 1933 but failed to make a career as a literary journalist. Suffering from psychosomatic problems in the wake of his father's death, he underwent psychoanalysis in London with the distinguished analyst W. R. Bion, but without much immediate benefit to his health. In retrospect, however, he thought the treatment 'helped me to understand a bit better what I was doing and what I was feeling' (qtd in Knowlson and Knowlson 2006, p. 68). It was in London that he wrote the novel *Murphy*. After travelling round Nazi Germany in 1936–37 (visiting art galleries and museums), he finally left Ireland to settle in Paris in 1937. There, in January 1938, having survived a near-fatal stabbing, he began living with the woman who was to become (although not until 1961) his wife, Suzanne Deschevaux-Dumesnil (1899–1989).

When war was declared in September 1939, Beckett was visiting his mother in Ireland. He returned to Paris immediately. After the fall of France, in June 1940, during the German occupation, he began to work for a Resistance cell. When the cell was betrayed in August 1942, many of its members were arrested, but Beckett escaped, together with Suzanne. They fled south, ending up in the village of Roussillon, in the Vaucluse region. There they worked picking grapes for a local vineyard. Beckett also laboured on a farm. In his free time he wrote the novel *Watt* (not published until 1953).

It has been plausibly suggested that the Roussillon experience informs *Godot* in a fundamental way: 'Hiding in the woods and fields, they [fugitives such as Beckett and Suzanne] never knew when they heard someone approach whether it would be a Nazi patrol or friendly villagers' (Gontarski 1985, p. 36; see also Knowlson 1996, pp. 380–1 and Kenner 1973, pp. 30–1). And the circumstances are explicitly – even disarmingly – alluded to in *En attendant Godot*, when Vladimir reminds Estragon in Act II (see Beckett 2006, p. 208) that they picked grapes for a man called Bonnelly at Roussillon. (In *Waiting for Godot* Vladimir has a lapse of memory at this point, and in both versions Estragon says he never noticed the remarkable red earth of the district.) This sudden naked outcrop of exact autobiographical detail (see Knowlson 1996, p. 323) amidst the carefully controlled referential landscape of the play is both unexpected and disconcerting. The reference is, as James Mays says, 'almost private, yet nothing is gained by sharing in that privacy' (1987, p. 163). If the English version is regarded as a revision, then it may be that Beckett thought better of the inclusion; but although the thematic reason for such a revision is absolutely clear (the passage is after all about remembering), the French text was never revised. Thus a formative, perhaps even originary, experience is allowed to leave its mark in at least one version of the text. Typically, the localizing gesture adds to, rather than dispels, our puzzlement.

After the liberation in 1944, Beckett returned to Paris, but by spring 1945 he was back in Dublin, seeing his mother and sorting out his financial affairs. He then returned to France as a volunteer worker (storekeeper and driver) in the establishment of an Irish Red Cross Hospital in Saint-Lô, Normandy, which had been 'bombed out of existence in one night' (Beckett 1995, p. 277) during the Allied invasion. This was, in Beckett's phrase (and the title of his only piece of reportage), 'the Capital of the Ruins'. But before his return, alone in his mother's room in Foxrock, he had experienced what he referred to as 'a vision' (see Knowlson 1996, pp. 351–3).

A version of this vision (though not a literal one) appears in the 1958 play, *Krapp's Last Tape*, the vision in the mother's room being there imaginatively rehandled in a play which circles around the death of the protagonist's mother. We can never know the substance of it, but its essence was clarified by statements Beckett made in interviews some years later. The vital point is his sharp awareness of the contrast between his own imaginative process and that of his literary 'father', James Joyce. He told Israel Shenker in 1956:

The kind of work I do is one in which I'm not master of my material. The more Joyce knew the more he could. He's tending toward omniscience and omnipotence as an artist. I'm working with impotence, ignorance. I don't think impotence has been exploited in the past. (Graver and Federman 1979, p. 148)

The authenticity of the Shenker interview is in doubt, but 33 years later, and less than two months before his death, Beckett spoke in similar terms to his authorized biographer, James Knowlson:

I realized that Joyce had gone as far as one could in the direction of knowing more, in control of one's material. [. . .] I realized that my own way was in impoverishment, in lack of knowledge and in taking away, subtracting rather than adding. (Knowlson and Knowlson 2006, p. 47)

In contrast to Joyce's plenitude, Beckett's art was to be one of inanition. This was a deliberate embracing of imaginative poverty, a *not* knowing, a *not* being able, which involved a paradoxical commitment to weakness and artistic failure. It is perhaps best understood (with reference to what we have already observed about *Waiting for Godot*) as a deliberate renunciation of conventional artistic means and resources. The means were to be renounced and the way was to be a negative one.

The effect of this commitment was remarkable. Joyce scholars have demurred at the falsification involved in 'the Joyce that Beckett built' (see Dettmar 1999), but the process of 'placing' his literary precursor in this way was profoundly necessary for Beckett. In what he himself described as a 'frenzy of writing' (qtd in Knowlson 1996, p. 358), in the parenthesis of time between the vision in his mother's room and the death of his mother in 1950, he produced four novels (including a trilogy), three novellas and two plays. 'They came in one great spurt of enthusiasm' (Graver and Federman 1979, p. 216). The second of the plays, written between 9 October 1948 and 29 January 1949, was the work which was instrumental in his being, in words he quoted from Alexander Pope, 'damned to fame'. This was *Waiting for Godot*.

Or rather, it was *En attendant Godot*. For all these texts were written in French, and often not translated until some years afterwards. A central part of the project of self-impoverishment was a very deliberate attempt to put aside the rich layers of association, connotation and allusion – literary and personal – normally experienced (more or less unconsciously) by speakers or writers using their native tongue. Again the way is negative. Beckett chose to write in French, he said, 'Parce qu'en français c'est plus facile d'écrire sans style' (qtd in Beckett 1966, p. xx) – because in French it is easier to write *without* style. It was, he said on another occasion, 'from a desire to impoverish myself still further [m'appauvrir encore davantage]. That was the real motive' (qtd in Janvier 1969, p. 18).

It needs to be noted, though, that the equation is far from neat. Beckett's first completed play, *Eleutheria* (the Greek word for freedom), was written in January and February 1947, also in French, and its means are far from impoverished. It concerns a young man alienated from his bourgeois family, and his refusal either to emerge from his solitary bedsit or to explain himself. It has 17 characters (including a prompter and a spectator who crosses from the auditorium), three acts, and (split) sets and (simultaneous) action intricate enough to require a three-page note from the author by way of clarification. Beckett released the text only reluctantly. It was published in 1995, and has yet to receive a professional production. It does indeed have anticipations of *Godot* and some later plays, but its extravagance of means casts the minimalism of the former into even sharper relief. The contrast shaped the fate of the two plays, for economy in the theatre is also (always) a matter of money. One reason for Roger Blin's decision to stage *Godot* rather than *Eleutheria* in 1953 was that a production of *Godot* would be so much cheaper. He said he found the play 'rich and unique in its nudity' (qtd in Aslan 1988, p. 23).

In Beckett's writings about art, of which there are several in the immediate post-war period, the metaphor of poverty recurs. Of his friends the brothers van Velde he wrote in 1948, 'their painting is the analysis of a state of privation' (1983, p. 136; my translation). In *Three Dialogues with Georges Duthuit* (1949) he speaks passionately of his 'dream of an art unresentful of its insuperable indigence and too proud for the farce of giving and receiving' (1983, p. 141), and expresses his scorn for artists who 'have turned wisely tail, before the ultimate penury' (1983, p. 143). Privation, indigence, penury. Poverty was never merely a metaphor for Beckett. In the post-war years the social reality was everywhere unignorable, and he himself knew well what it was to be (in the words of one of his favourite writers, Samuel Johnson), 'oppressed with want' (1984, p. 163). However in these instances from his art criticism, as in his statements explaining why he chose to write in French, poverty is a metaphor for a certain attitude towards the creative process.

This attitude is one which conceives of the condition of being as profoundly problematic, and regards creativity as an authentic confrontation of it – at a particular time, and in a particular place. It is implied that this is a matter of choice: artists can refuse the obligation, but if they do so they are deceiving themselves, because (as we shall see) the state of being involves processes which are themselves unavoidably creative. In Beckett's view, the artistic process enacts a stripping or an exfoliation, in an attempt to reach what his younger self termed 'the ideal core of the onion'. 'The only fertile research' he wrote in 1931, 'is excavatory, immersive, a contraction of the spirit, a descent' (1965a, pp. 29, 65). This mining inwards towards a heart that is 'ideal' because it is non-existent (like that of the onion) is the progression enacted by the three novels – usually referred to as a trilogy – that Beckett wrote between 1947 and 1950. In *Molloy*, the vagrant Molloy is unsuccessfully tracked by the private detective Moran as he makes his way towards his mother. Molloy ends in a ditch, and when Moran returns home, coming more and more to resemble his quarry, he is bereft of domestic comforts yet strangely calm. Each man is required by mysterious others to tell his own story. In *Malone meurt* (*Malone Dies*) an old man tells himself stories about others which gradually converge on and merge with his own life even as he dies. In *L'Innommable* (*The Unnamable*) the narrator is reduced to a voice projecting a series of avatars, his 'vice-exister[s]' (1959, p. 317), which enable him, in increasing desperation, to carry on speaking even as he yearns to stop for ever. He perceives, or imagines himself, orbited by either

Malone or Molloy or both, as though he were the centre of a
planetary system. Yet he is a centre that resists definition and
finally dissolves into the centrifugal motion of contradictory
needs and energies: 'where I am, I don't know, I'll never know, in
the silence you don't know, you must go on, I can't go on, I'll go
on' (1959, p. 418). This third novel brought, said Beckett, 'complete disintegration': '[it] landed me in a situation I can't extricate
myself from' (Graver and Federman 1979, pp. 148, 149).

Then: 'I began to write *Godot* as a relaxation, to get away from
the awful prose I was writing at that time' (qtd in Beckett 1966,
p. xlv). 'I just thought I would try it out' (qtd in Duckworth 1972,
p. 17). In fact the play was written after *Malone meurt* and before
L'Innommable. That it was written quickly (in less than 15 weeks)
and apparently without any major impediment would support
the author's statement, at least in relation to its initial drafting.
It is an attractive irony: the century's most famous play as a swift
diversion – not quite an afterthought, but nonetheless an in-
between-thought. Yet the play, relaxation or not, is recognizably
part of the same artistic project as the novel trilogy. The medium
of theatre was at once a relief from prose and an opportunity to
continue the project in other terms – and with(out) other means.

Let us return to my suggestion of *Godot* as an exercise in self-
impoverishment. As we've seen, the dramatic means and materials are minimized. That Vladimir and Estragon cannot leave the
stage is almost (though not quite) a rule. They are given virtually
nothing to do (which is why there is 'nothing to be done') and not
much to do it with. Put another way, they could do *anything*, but
that, because it wouldn't cause Godot to come any sooner,
wouldn't make any difference either. (So much for freedom.)
Pozzo and Lucky arrive ('Reinforcements at last!' (p. 77)), but
reasons have to be found for them to stay for a while, because the
rule is that these two must move on. The Boy turns up at the end
of each act to ensure that the men don't conclude that Godot
simply doesn't exist. Thus the Boy compels their continuing presence ('Hope deferred . . .'). Nightfall, weirdly immediate and
right on cue, relieves the urgency of their obligation but does not
remove it. They *could* move, but 'they do not move' (pp. 54, 94).
The playwright therefore minimizes his characters' means even

as he minimizes his own. What this confronts them with is clear from the very beginning. The play's first joke is one of its best, partly because it is also an explicit, serious statement of theme:

> VLADIMIR: So there you are again.
> ESTRAGON: Am I?
>
> (p. 9)

In a seminal early response to the play, Beckett's fellow novelist Alain Robbe-Grillet made this point, and in doing so indicated the true originality of *Godot*:

> We suddenly realize, as we look at them, the main function of theatre, which is to show what the fact of *being there* consists in. For this is what we have never seen on the stage before, or not with the same clarity, not with so few concessions and so much force. (1965, p. 113)

Presence: Vladimir and Estragon, as everyone knows, can't absent themselves. But nor can they experience themselves as fully present. Waiting is a kind of suspension, and here it presses, and oppresses, beyond boredom. Language itself can't *quite* cope with this sensation, and comedy is the result:

> VLADIMIR: I'm glad to see you back. I thought you were
> gone for ever.
> ESTRAGON: Me too.
>
> (p. 9)

By what means, then, does the escapologist playwright untie his own hands? And what do these means have to do with the matter of presence in the theatre? It is in order to address these problems that I now turn to the question of character in *Waiting for Godot*.

CHARACTER AND PATTERN

A glance at the history of criticism about *Godot* serves to confirm a strong first impression: there are several features which have made this play compulsively interesting to scholars and critics, but character is not one of them.

The first French responses to *En attendant Godot* stressed the mixture of clown-like humour and philosophical gravity (see Graver and Federman 1979, pp. 88–92 and Cohn 1987, pp. 24–8). This was a 'metaphysical farce', it was clear. In Britain, allegorical explanations were attempted; religious resonances seemed irresistible and debate about meaning became vigorous (see Graver and Federman 1979, pp. 93–104). The first academic critics focused either on philosophy or on language and style, and the best ones wrote about the relation between these features (see, for example, essays in Esslin 1965, and various studies by Ruby Cohn and Hugh Kenner). There was no major shift in focus in the 1970s, though studies of influence and scrutiny of dramaturgy and performance significantly extended the critical view. But *Waiting for Godot* afforded little interest for conventional critical approaches to character because questions of individual motive in the play are relatively unimportant – or, more to the point, relatively uncomplicated. The play has plenty of puzzles, but these, by and large, don't involve the reasons why this or that character behaves in a particular way. We aren't led to expect 'complex', 'rounded' characters, and we don't get them. Not even the shallowest spectator (or critic) ever complained that Vladimir and Estragon weren't interesting in the way Hamlet or Hedda Gabler are interesting. From the outset it was always clear that the interest lay not in the depth of either of them (or of Pozzo and Lucky) but in the connection *between* them. We may invent pasts for the individual characters – and indeed certain details could even be said to invite us to do this. If we are actors, we may regard such invention as a necessary way of working towards the end that is performance. But ultimately that is our business: the text of the play, even if it occasionally teases us, gives us no confirmation, no resolution. Thus, as far as character was concerned, criticism noted the distinguishing features of these figures and showed how they interacted or interlocked, one with the other. Moral considerations were frequently raised – that is, how as individuals they respond to one another and to their situation. However, the mode of characterization (in conventional terms, pretty 'flat') was normally seen as being an essential part of Beckett's philosophical vision of the human condition, which was certainly not primarily concerned with individual motive.

Then came literary theory. Yet whatever significant shifts were made by deconstruction, psychoanalysis, feminism, reader-centred criticism and other approaches, they were not in the direction of character. The fundamental emphasis of any form of theory, on character as a *construction* within a literary or cultural context rather than a more or less truthful imitation of life, might have been expected to prompt work on *Godot*. Here, after all, the constructedness of the characters is so evident that the characters themselves often seem conscious of their own artificiality. Work was indeed forthcoming, but the very self-consciousness which is so attractive to the postmodern mind itself presents a problem to criticism.

Consider the following much-quoted passage of dialogue from Act I. Pozzo has lost his pipe:

POZZO: What have I done with my pipe?
VLADIMIR: Charming evening we're having.
ESTRAGON: Unforgettable.
VLADIMIR: And it's not over.
ESTRAGON: Apparently not.
VLADIMIR: It's only beginning.
ESTRAGON: It's awful.
VLADIMIR: Worse than the pantomime.
ESTRAGON: The circus.
VLADIMIR: The music-hall.
ESTRAGON: The circus.
POZZO: What can I have done with that briar?
ESTRAGON: He's a scream. He's lost his dudeen.
    Laughs noisily.
VLADIMIR: I'll be back.
    He hastens towards the wings.
ESTRAGON: End of the corridor, on the left.
VLADIMIR: Keep my seat.
    Exit Vladimir.

(pp. 34–5)

Like many of the play's funnier moments, it is a moment of *metatheatre* – a moment of theatre *about* theatre, performance which makes reference to performance – and one that deliberately confuses the levels of fiction and reality. As Vladimir and Estragon exchange comments on the show, the very medium of their comments – swift comic cross-talk – is recognizable as deriving from the forms of entertainment they mention, and these forms are referred to with typical comic self-disparagement. When Vladimir's bladder problem forces his exit, Estragon directs him not to an appropriately bushy spot offstage near the country road which is their fictional location, but to the backstage toilet of the theatre in which these actors, all four of them, are performing. Vladimir's parting shot ('Keep my seat') puts him and Estragon in the audience with us, and further points to Pozzo as a performer ('He's a scream'). Indeed, everyone is being cast in a role. It's the confusion of levels that makes it all funny. But the critic is left with a problem as inescapable as Vladimir's bladder. Our subjects have done our work for us: they have drawn attention to their own artificiality – their stylistic origins and their mode of existence. Just in case we hadn't noticed. As Richard Keller Simon has noted, 'in a curiously comic way *Godot* plays a game with its critics by anticipating their obvious responses, and confounding them' (1987, p. 112). What Eric Bentley identified as the play's 'parody of the dramatic' (1987, p. 24) is simultaneously a parody, in advance, of the critical. Why should the critic labour the point the play so deftly makes about itself? Accordingly, discussion of character as construction dissolves, flowing smoothly into analysis of the operations of metatheatre, of language games and performance, and the cultural implications of these. From the beginning, critical attention to *Godot* had always been preoccupied with patterns of different kinds – verbal and visual. Now theory, recognizing the play's comic recognition of its own artificiality, has confirmed and further justified this preoccupation.

Such critical moves are understandable, and often lead to insightful readings. My own approach to the play is heavily indebted to them, as will become apparent. Nonetheless, as both readers and spectators, our responses on a very basic and important level are to characters. To discount these responses would be as counter-productive as to espouse them exclusively. At the very least we need to be aware of the possibility for more traditional readings of character. Consider, for example, this passage from the end of Act I, as the men interrogate Mr Godot's Boy:

> VLADIMIR: Do you belong to these parts?
> BOY: Yes, sir.
> ESTRAGON: That's all a pack of lies. (*Shaking the Boy by the arm.*) Tell us the truth.
> BOY: (*trembling*). But it is the truth, sir!
> VLADIMIR: Will you let him alone! What's the matter with you? (*Estragon releases the Boy, moves away, covering his face with his hands. Vladimir and the Boy observe him. Estragon drops his hands. His face is convulsed.*) What's the matter with you?
> ESTRAGON: I'm unhappy.
> VLADIMIR: Not really! Since when?
> ESTRAGON: I'd forgotten.
> VLADIMIR: Extraordinary the tricks that memory plays! (*Estragon tries to speak, renounces, limps to his place, sits down and begins to take off his boots.*)
>
> (p. 50)

Estragon's anguish takes its place within a pattern of behaviour and response. Vladimir's sarcasm (for so it is) prompts the oddity of Estragon's retort: he had forgotten he was unhappy! Then Vladimir's summary comment relates the moment to the play's other instances of failing or uncertain memory. Even here, the music hall is not so far away. But the most noticeable feature of the passage is the disparity between the 'convulsed' face and 'I'm unhappy' as a verbal gesture which can hardly compass or express Estragon's despair. (Interestingly, when directing the play Beckett simplified this moment by dropping the hand-gestures.) It is a genuinely emotional moment, and the humour of the verbal exchange serves only to intensify it. The actor needs to carry these intense feelings of unhappiness through his subsequent drowse on the stone to his awakening, two pages later, when they have settled into a placid self-pity. On waking, after the departure of the Boy, Estragon arranges his boots on the ground, leaving them for someone else, 'with smaller feet'. He contemplates the moon and (mis)quotes P. B. Shelley, seemingly drained. Yet in the ensuing exchange, the spit of resentment is still there:

VLADIMIR: But you can't go barefoot!
ESTRAGON: Christ did.
VLADIMIR: Christ! What's Christ got to do with it? You're not going to compare yourself to Christ!
ESTRAGON: All my life I've compared myself to him.
VLADIMIR: But where he lived it was warm, it was dry!
ESTRAGON: Yes. And they crucified quick.

(p. 52)

There is a satisfying psychological continuity in this little (unfinished) sequence for Estragon: from anger to declared unhappiness through brief oblivion and then to ruminative self-pity and renewed resentment. It has to be articulated across the gap of his drowse, while Vladimir questions the Boy. It is one that any competent actor would recognize as being necessary to project, as it falls squarely within a conventional psychological articulation of role. In other words, there is a character here, behaving as plausibly and as recognizably as any character in a Chekhov play. Elsewhere, and even at the same time, Estragon is part of a larger pattern of dialogue which is characterized by metatheatre and language games, but our understanding of him, as of the other characters, needs equally to be informed by considerations of this more traditional kind.

Thus, if *Waiting for Godot* disturbs or interrupts our settled way of reading character – as it certainly does – it can hardly be said to dissolve it unproblematically into pattern and form and metatheatrical abstraction. As we shall see in later chapters, just as the characters of the play, whether waiting or travelling, exist, and feel themselves to exist, in a state of suspension, so their status as literary and theatrical characters can be described in the same terms: they are positioned, strangely, *between* individuality and stylization, between relatedness and independence, between pattern and autonomy, between 'flat' and 'round', between surface and depth, partaking of opposite spheres but never fully classifiable within either.

For the purposes of our critical observation, this means that distinctions between characters, their individual markers – the way they speak, what they wear, the way they move or situate themselves on the stage – are themselves essential parts of the many patterns which are perceptible throughout the action. One of our tasks will be to recognize how at any given moment in the play the individual character relates to a variety of potential or implicit patterns – textual, spatial, performative, or stylistic. Considerations of character and pattern need to be simultaneously present to our minds.

Quite how *explicit* different patterns are made in the play depends on the degree and kind of detail provided by the play text. In fact it depends upon the accuracy and consistency of the detail provided by the text being used, whether in the study or as the script for performance. It is to these issues – issues related to the correctness of the printed text and to different versions of the play – that I now turn.

THREE EDITIONS

When he directed *Godot* in 1975, or advised on later productions, Beckett took the opportunity to revise the play text, around 30 years after writing it. He thought the existing texts 'a mess' because he considered he had not visualized the play thoroughly enough while writing it. 'You should visualise every action of your characters', he wrote to a friend. 'Know precisely in what direction they are speaking. Know the pauses' (qtd in McMillan and Fehsenfeld 1988, p. 16). In fact, as McMillan and Fehsenfeld remark, Beckett's notebook for his Berlin production 'makes many points that are only implicit in the original play definite and explicit' (1988, p. 135). Nonetheless it is a pardonable exaggeration, which highlights the question of the degree of control the playwright should expect to exert over the production of a play. No question has been more vexing than this one in the production history of *Godot*, and it is one to which I shall return shortly.

However there is another, and much more accurate, sense in which the text of the play is a mess. When Beckett told James Knowlson that 'I know my texts are in a terrible mess' (qtd in Knowlson 1999, p. 176), he was referring to errors in and anomalies between printed versions of the same play. *Godot* is a good example. The situation is neatly summarized by S. E. Gontarski in his Introduction to the latest of the three editions of the play which together form essential reference for the student. This is the bilingual edition of *En attendant Godot* / *Waiting for Godot* published by Grove Press on the centenary of the author's birth. For the English-speaking student with any French at all, this book, or the bilingual edition brought out by Beckett's British publisher Faber and Faber in the same year, is an invaluable supplement, if not a necessity. The Faber bilingual edition supplements (and reproduces) the standard Faber text of the play, which was first published in 1965. This text was announced as 'definitive', replacing as it did the first Faber edition of 1956, which was bowdlerized according to the demands of the Lord Chamberlain, by whom, up to 1968, all scripts were required by law to be approved for public performance. (Beckett referred to him as 'the Lord Chamberpot' (Harmon 1998, p. 24).) Thus, for example, for Vladimir's Act II fear that if Lucky 'get[s] going all of a sudden [. . .] we'd be ballocksed' (p. 79), the first edition has 'banjaxed' (Beckett 1986, p. 79). (The alteration at least has the merit of recognizing an Irish turn of phrase: the English say 'buggered'.) The student in the UK will in all probability be studying the 1965 edition of the play. It is the one normally referred to throughout this book (see my note at the end of this Introduction).

'Definitive', however, would not seem to be the right word for it. Knowlson (1999, p. 177) notes significant differences between Faber 1965 and the standard American edition (Grove Press, 1954), and although Gontarski claims that the Grove bilingual brings 'British and American texts closer to harmony' (Beckett 2006, p. viii), these differences are still there. In fact these are errors in the Grove; nonetheless we can still echo the question asked by Hersh Zeifman in the most authoritative study of the play's texts:

Is it not bizarre . . . that this arguably most famous and significant work of the post-war English theatre – and certainly the most analysed in scholarly periodicals – should exist in one form for a British audience and in another, somewhat different form for an American one? (1987, p. 93)

(A *caveat* should be entered against Faber's first hardback edition of *The Complete Dramatic Works*, published in 1986, as for some strange reason the text of *Godot* printed there is that of the expurgated first edition. The first paperback edition of the *Complete*, published in 1998, reverts to the 1965 edition.)

In 1993, Faber in the UK, and Grove in the USA, printed an extensively 'revised text', together with facsimiles and transcriptions of the theatrical notebooks Beckett compiled in preparation for his production of *Warten auf Godot* at the Schiller-Theater, Berlin in 1975. The extensive notes and full scholarly apparatus by Dougald McMillan and James Knowlson make this volume an indispensable scholarly resource (though, at the time of writing, it is very expensive and not easy to obtain). Yet it is hard to feel that this edition finally resolves the textual problem surrounding *Waiting for Godot*. It may even add another dimension to that problem.

The revised text is based not only on Beckett's Schiller-Theater production but on the 'two English-language adaptations' (McMillan and Knowlson 1993, p. 3) of that production by American companies. The editors emphasize the 'large degree of consensus' between the productions. (The two American ones were prepared by Beckett's German assistant, Walter Asmus.) There are significant cuts, and a great many alterations and additions to stage directions, indicating Beckett's near-choreographic approach as a director. 'The resulting "revised text" ', the editors state, 'may be regarded as a new version of *Godot*, shorter, tighter in structure, and visualized much more clearly in theatrical terms, as well as being, in our view, aesthetically more satisfying' (McMillan and Knowlson 1993, p. xii). The 1975 production can indeed be thought of as a text in itself. '[T]he German *Godot*', Ciaran Ross has suggested, 'may be said to unwittingly form a "Ghost" trilogy with *Footfalls* and *That Time*, two plays written around the same time' (2001, p. 64). In Ross's reading the Beckett of 1975 both revisits and re-imagines the work of 1948–49, in the light of the plays he was writing and staging at the same time.

It is the editors' value-judgement concerning the revised text that gives one pause: 'aesthetically more satisfying'. One may indeed agree, but it is this move that prevents us from settling with the many possible literary parallels: Wordsworth's *Prelude*, of 1799, 1805 and 1850; Coleridge's obsessive self-revision; Pope's *Dunciad*, the Variorum and the 'new'; late and early Auden; Shakespeare's *Hamlet* and *King Lear*. The post-theoretical interest in what is usually referred to as the 'instability' of the literary text, or the relatively recent emphasis on the provisional status of the written text within the theatre: these trends make such texts extremely attractive, and *Waiting for Godot* might be added to the list. But where the scholar can hold a plurality of texts in view for the purposes of analysis, the theatre-practitioner has to make commitments and choices for the sake of performance. The scholar can examine the relation between the Quarto *History of King Lear* (1608) and the Folio *Tragedy of King Lear* (1623), making the case for their being essentially different plays, the latter a radical revision of the former; but director and actors must choose one or the other, or the traditional conflation of the two. The case of the 'old' and 'new' *Godot*s is a similar one.

This is where value-judgements enter in. The traditionalist, in the shape of Colin Duckworth, agrees that 'we now have a different play', expressing a 'vision [. . .] of a greyer world, glimpsed through the filter of his later works'. He agrees that 'it is an incomparable barometer of the evolution of the Beckettian world view over thirty years'. But he still sees it as the result of 'textual vandalism': 'it makes one wonder whether authors should be let loose on their plays thirty-odd years later'. Above all, he preserves the idea of an 'original', of which the revised text is deemed 'an impoverishment' (1987, pp. 190–1). In fact his approach is not essentially different from that of the editors of the revised text: in both cases an original is posed against a revision. It is simply that what they see as 'aesthetically more satisfying', he regards as an 'aberration'.

Itself technically a conflation (following from productions with three different companies), the revised text is at the very least an extraordinary, perhaps unique, printed record of a conception of a play, modified (sometimes significantly) by circumstances of performance. Bertolt Brecht compiled 'model-books' for productions of three of his plays, but these consisted essentially of sequences of still photographs, rather than texts with enormously detailed stage directions. Such texts of course raise in its most unignorable form the problem of the playwright's authority over the performance of his own script. All the evidence points to the fact that Beckett wanted his play to be staged in accordance with the cuts and additions and alterations enshrined in the revised text. Its very existence implies its status as prescription rather then merely description. And however contentious the issue of cuts, the more interesting problem, it seems to me, lies in the additional stage directions. These imply a performance style, and indeed a whole way of working, which actors from different performance traditions would find problematic, if not actually alien. Furthermore, they can hardly be regarded as marginal, as Beckett always opined that his move to drama was occasioned to begin with by the 'relaxing' attractions of stage-space and the opportunities for authorial control that it afforded: 'I felt the need to create for a smaller space, one in which I had some control of where people stood or moved'; 'You have a definite space and people in this space. That's relaxing' (qtd in McMillan and Fehsenfeld 1988, p. 15).

For our purposes, however, the revised text, and the notebooks from which it largely derives, together constitute a rich resource. This is not – emphatically not – because it contains some definitive 'final' indication of how characters are to be conceived, or what the play means, but because its departures from the standard text, whether these are considered improvements or aberrations, often enable us to focus what is at stake in particular performance options. As these options bear importantly upon the relation between character and pattern which I highlighted earlier, and as they inevitably involve alternative conceptions of character, we shall be returning to the revised text often in our discussions of Vladimir and Estragon, and Pozzo and Lucky.

Before moving to the characters, though, I shall consider in Chapter 1 some of the puzzles and difficulties associated with *Godot*, and how these might condition our reading. Then, in Chapter 2, I shall discuss not character as such, but an essential element for our understanding of its nature in this play: the dominant pattern of relationship in which the characters are fixed.

Note: Unless otherwise indicated, quotations from *Waiting for Godot* are from the second edition, published by Faber and Faber in 1965. At certain points in my discussion, I quote extensively from the revised text of the play, published by Faber and Faber with *The Theatrical Notebooks of Samuel Beckett, Vol. 1* in 1993 (see above). For the sake of clarity, in the chapters that follow, I have prefaced quotations from the revised text and its editors' notes with '1993'.

CHAPTER 1

PUZZLES AND DIFFICULTIES

It is an irresistible truism: *Waiting for Godot* is a difficult play. Even defining the difficulty isn't straightforward. To call the play 'deceptively simple' (Scherzer 1991, p. 90) is to suggest a booby trap. But in any case, it is reported that 'students and theatregoers who initially approach Beckett's work unawares are typically frustrated by its plotlessness and the obliquity of its themes' (Hutchings 1991, p. 26). Or perhaps students, like the prisoners in San Quentin in 1957 who constituted the play's single most famous audience, are 'without any preconceived theatrical expectations or theories and so [. . .] not troubled by the lack of plot, action, or realistic behaviour' (Zinman 1991, p. 152). Is it the case that this is 'a play particularly accessible to students because it depicts the world in which they live and expresses an attitude toward that world to which they can immediately relate' (Ben-Zvi 1991, p. 37)? Or conversely that 'when students confront Beckett's drama, which is so [. . .] antagonistic to traditional dramaturgical values, their frustration often resembles Gogo's: "Nothing happens, nobody comes, nobody goes, it's awful!"' (Garner 1991, p. 141)?

Audiences, and students, are blessedly different, of course – from place to place and from generation to generation. Nevertheless, as Wordsworth asserted, 'every author, as far as he is great and at the same time *original*, has had the task of *creating* the taste by which he is to be enjoyed' (1988, p. 408). In Beckett's case this might involve the cultivation of, in the words (which impressed him) of another Romantic poet, '*Negative*

Capability, that is, when a man is capable of being in uncertainties, mysteries, doubts, without any irritable reaching after fact and reason' (Keats 1947, p. 72). And if the evidence of one scholar-teacher is anything to go by, this taste has been created very successfully:

> it is not unusual to be informed even by one's undergraduate students that the question of Godot's identity is finally irrelevant to a 'correct' reading of the play, indeed, that this correctness is a function of refraining from so naïve a procedure as speculation on the absent character's identity. So much for the innocent audience. (Chaudhuri 1991, p. 135)

After such knowledge, what forgiveness for those still asking, 'Who is Godot?' Yet is this situation all gain? 'Twenty years ago', wrote one reviewer in 1977, 'when the play was new, everyone was trying to figure out what it meant, and it all had to be a symbol of something else. Here [in this production] the question of meaning never comes up. Like any good story, it means itself' (qtd in Croall 2005, p. 102). But what does 'it means itself' *mean*? And does not worrying about meaning equate with 'understanding', or even with the best form of appreciation?

Several statements by the author suggest that he would think so, but in this area it is important to discriminate between exasperated dismissals and helpful pointers. The famous response to 'Who or what does Godot mean?' – 'If I knew, I would have said so in the play' (qtd in Graver and Federman 1979, p. 177) – is robustly truthful, and indeed rather helpful, where 'I produce an object. What people make of it is not my concern' (qtd in Beckett 1966, p. xxiv) seems merely surly. Much more interesting is the statement of 1956, reported by Alec Reid, that 'the great success of *Waiting for Godot* had arisen from a misunderstanding: critics and public alike were busy interpreting in allegorical or symbolic terms a play which strove at all cost to avoid definition' (qtd in Beckett 1966, p. xcvii). The metaphor of activity ('strove [. . .] to avoid') at least avoids the suggestion that the play is an innocent, well-meaning victim of its interpreters. In doing so it indicates that interpretation is not (or not just) something that is 'done to' the play, but something the play itself is actively concerned with – in its processes and perhaps also as theme. I have already referred, in my Introduction, to the conditions for these dramatic processes. A crucial effect of the minimization of means which we noted is that nothing is ever, in the inspired phrase of Bert O. States, 'reliably insignificant'. States continues:

> in a text so spare, so cunningly random, everything is a lure. Well and good for Beckett to insist there are no symbols where none are intended, but he himself (like a boy who failed to cry wolf) has set the conditions whereby all images, the more off-handed the more suspicious, loom as potential motifs in the grand design. (1978, p. 31)

We can see the process described by States at work early on in the play, when Vladimir seeks to remind Estragon of 'Two thieves, crucified at the same time as our Saviour. [. . .] One is supposed to have been saved and the other . . . [. . .] damned' (p. 12). The ensuing exchange covers two pages of script. A teacher would be right to ask students 'why Beckett would include this material so early in the play' (Simpson 1991, p. 81). The question is a leading one, no doubt (as such questions usually are), but nonetheless necessary for that. The Christian framework, the two thieves, two boots, two men waiting in a state of unknowingness. Beckett himself was preoccupied with the case:

> I am interested in the shape of ideas even if I do not believe in them. There is a wonderful sentence in Augustine. [. . .] 'Do not despair; one of the thieves was saved. Do not presume; one of the thieves was damned'. That sentence has a wonderful shape. It is the shape that matters. (qtd in States 1978, p. viii)

Although the wonderful sentence is in fact not to be found in Augustine (see Ackerley and Gontarski 2004, p. 593), the 'shape' idea is nonetheless a key one, and is recognized as such by States, and by many other critics. This famous statement is indeed essential, but it is also a feint by Beckett – disingenuous and perhaps even provocative. It is as though the shape mattered to the virtual exclusion of the content. Even in the play, it might be claimed, the exchange about the thieves is chiefly material for another cross-talk 'canter':

> VLADIMIR: Come on, Gogo, return the ball, can't you, once in a way?
> ESTRAGON: (*with exaggerated enthusiasm*). I find this really most extraordinarily interesting.

(pp. 12–13)

And then Vladimir returns to the testimony of the Evangelists. The Boy may fail to cry wolf (as States says), but the wolf is now firmly installed at the door labelled Meaning. We are being dared by the play to ignore it.

The more off-handed the image in this play, reckons States, the more suspicious for those seeking meaning. Let us consider what is probably the *least* off-handed of the play's images, and its effect in and on the 'grand design' (if there is one).

GOD AND *GODOT*

This is not the place for another survey of who or what Godot may be (see, for example, Beckett 1966, pp. cxiii–cxvi, Graver 2004, pp. 41–2 and Ackerley and Gontarski 2004, pp. 231–2). A good working formulation is provided by Lawrence Graver: 'for us at least if not for the two men on the road, Godot has become a concept – an idea of promise and expectation – of that for which people aware of the absence of coherent meaning in their lives wait in the hope that it will restore significance to their existence' (2004, p. 40). As many critics have rightly pointed out, when Estragon 'does the tree' in Act II and asks, 'Do you think God sees me?' (p. 76), he speaks of God as a 'given', as a culturally-shared idea quite distinct from Godot. (The tree is a yoga position. 'It is the hands pressed together as though in prayer that produces Estragon's question', Beckett explained to Peter Hall, his first British director, see Harmon 1998, p. 4.) And when immediately afterwards he cries out, 'God have pity on me!' (p. 77), he is not addressing someone who might just turn up at any minute. An extremely irritated Beckett told Ralph Richardson 'that if by Godot I had meant God I would [have] said God, and not Godot' (qtd in Knowlson 1996, p. 412). Yet though sophisticated students might think it naïve to identify Godot with God, it would be equally naïve to pretend that the play does not invite the identification. As Bert O. States wittily puts it: 'God is not absent from the play; he is simply not quite present' (1978, p. 60).

The Boy who appears at the end of each act is Mr Godot's messenger and therefore the men's only source of information about him. At the end of Act I, the Boy tells Vladimir that he minds the goats for Godot, and that his brother minds the sheep. In Jesus' parable in Matthew 25:31–46, the blessed (sheep) are separated from the damned (goats). (As we have just seen, the motif of salvation and damnation has been introduced early into the play by Vladimir's obsession with the two thieves crucified with Jesus.) In *Godot* it is the shepherd-brother who is beaten, not the one who is talking to Vladimir. The Boy does not know why. In Act II the Boy (usually the same actor, if not the same boy) tells Vladimir that Mr Godot has a white beard (he thinks), and Vladimir responds with 'Christ have mercy on us!' (p. 92). The white beard picks up the traditional view of the Old Testament God heard at the beginning of Lucky's Act I Think: 'a personal God [. . .] with white beard [. . .] outside time without extension who [. . .] loves us dearly with some exceptions for reasons unknown but time will tell and suffers [. . .] with those who [. . .] are plunged in torment plunged in fire' (pp. 42–3). At the very end of the play, having learned that Mr Godot 'does nothing' and has a white beard, Vladimir is more confident than he has been before about their situation. To Estragon's inquiry about what Godot would do if they 'dropped him', he replies, 'He'd punish us' (p. 93). 'And if he comes?' 'We'll be saved' (p. 94). For him, as for us, the word saved is now charged with Christian connotation. Before any of the critics, the first person who identified Godot with God was Vladimir.

Let us look again at Vladimir's question to the Boy about Godot's beard. It comes out of the blue and is entirely arbitrary (the Boy has just said that his brother is sick):

VLADIMIR: (*softly*). Has he a beard, Mr. Godot?
BOY: Yes, sir.
VLADIMIR: Fair or . . . (*he hesitates*) . . . or black?
BOY: I think it's white, sir.
   Silence.
VLADIMIR: Christ have mercy on us!
   Silence.

(p. 92)

The disparity between 'fair' and 'white' (also there in the French 'blonde' / 'blanche') is enough to assure him, and us too, that his question doesn't *merely* lead the Boy. But the hushed delivery and silences are enough to indicate the intensity of expectation that brushes aside the vagueness of the reply and produces Vladimir's *kyrie*. Is he merely deluded? No. Nonetheless one recognizes the moment as a vital insight into the dynamics of hope rather than the identity of Godot.

It is a moment that requires careful handling in production. The first English production, by Peter Hall in 1955, treated it, in the playwright's own phrase, with 'Anglican fervour' (qtd in Knowlson 1996, p. 417). At 'Christ have mercy on us!' Vladimir (Paul Daneman) removed his hat. Among the notes Beckett sent to Hall in a letter was: '*Christ have mercy on us*. Almost unintelligible ejaculation. Keep hat on' (Harmon 1998, p. 5). Nothing was to be given away – least of all to an audience which was prone to Christian interpretation. (At a comparable moment in Act I, when informing Vladimir that he slept in the loft (p. 51), the Boy pointed upwards. Beckett's note to Hall reads: 'Simply. No pointing to heaven' (Harmon 1998, p. 4).)

In his Berlin production Beckett added a third colour to Vladimir's inquiry: 'Fair or . . . (*he hesitates*) . . . or black . . . (*he hesitates*) . . . or red?' (1993, p. 83). This addition recalls, the editors of the revised text point out, 'the joke in the first act about the Englishman and the red-headed prostitute [p. 16]. By associating Godot with a flamboyant object of desire, it undercuts the suggestions of him as a God-like figure with a white beard' (1993, p. 170). But is the note of whimsy Vladimir's as well as the playwright's? The softness of utterance, the hesitations, the

33

silences remain. If, regarding Godot, '[e]verything is possible' (1993, p. 170), as Beckett's German translator remarked of the revision, then Vladimir is likely to find the Boy's answer *more* rather than less of a confirmation. Our recognition of the prostitute echo distances us slightly more from Vladimir: we can hear the echo, and perceive the pattern, where he cannot. Our sense of him as victim of his own desires and assumptions is tightened.

Godot offers the identification of Godot and God, to us as to Vladimir and Estragon. But even as it offers, it takes away. For what it offers is a parodic version of God – the Old Testament personal God with white beard, like William Blake's 'Nobodaddy', Nobody-Daddy. (As Hamm says in Beckett's next stage-play after this one, *Endgame*, 'The bastard! He doesn't exist!' (Beckett 1986, p. 119).) We are not naïve enough to swallow that, we say; but we find ourselves trying out the idea anyway. Beckett's often-quoted statement, 'Christianity is a mythology with which I am perfectly familiar, so I naturally use it' (qtd in Beckett 1966, p. lvii) is a provocative deadpan joke. Use it he certainly does, allowing his audience to experience a similar suspension of meaning to that lived out by his characters. Similar, but not the same. We see the trend of Vladimir's questioning, and we share his predicament enough to sympathize with what drives him. The Boy's response to the question about what Godot *does* – 'He does nothing, sir' (p. 91) – is indeed a thrillingly resonant moment, as has often been noticed, and it is so because of our momentary urge to identify Godot with God. But we are almost immediately distanced from Vladimir by our recognition of the very irresistibility of his desire to do the same. In the *Godot* world things are just not that clear, but his need has momentarily led him to forget that. His forgetting reminds us.

The last point is of capital importance. If Beckett's purpose was 'to give artistic expression to [. . .] the irrational state of unknowingness wherein we exist' (qtd in Graver 2004, p. 18), his 'dramatization of what it is like and what it means to exist in a state of radical unknowingness' (Graver 2004, p. 22) is important not just for its representation of characters in a particular predicament, but for the way it shapes the responses of the audience to these characters and their predicament. That '*Godot* involves the spectators in a process of waiting that doubles and repeats the waiting of the characters themselves' (Brewer 1987, p. 152) is a critical commonplace almost as old as the play itself. 'Beckett's refusal to give us firm answers to [. . .] questions is, of course, his way of putting his audience in the same universe – intellectually, emotionally, spiritually – that his characters inhabit' (Simpson 1991, p. 82). We can further examine how this universe is constructed, and how we are positioned in relation to it and the characters it contains, by looking at references to time and acts of memory in the play.

TIME AND MEMORY

'The laws of memory', wrote Beckett in his 1931 study of Marcel Proust, 'are subject to the more general laws of habit'; memory and habit being alike 'attributes of the Time cancer' (1965a, p. 18). In their attempts to evade 'the poisonous ingenuity of Time in the science of affliction' (1965a, p. 15), memory and habit end up refining it. *Waiting for Godot* restates the irony, but in terms which enable us to perceive its comedy as well as its tragedy. Vladimir is tormented by half-remembering; Estragon is less concerned to remember, and usually doesn't. Pozzo is no help: he remembers irrelevancies, which are nothing to do with them. Nor is Lucky, who remembers, in an overwhelming rush, nothing but 'sports of all sorts' (p. 43) and recondite fragments from an obsolete world of learning, making them all suffer more. In Act II they struggle to remember or remind themselves and each other of Act I: the play's bad memory (as it were) includes its not remembering itself.

For us, the effect is cumulative, and so sequence must be respected in our observations. What we notice are references, and memories, which either compress or elongate time in our perceptions. So in the first allusion to suicide (a missed opportunity): 'We should have thought of it a million years ago, in the nineties. [. . .] Hand in hand from the top of the Eiffel Tower, among the first' (p. 10). The dates work out plausibly: the Eiffel Tower was built in the 1890s; it is now the late 1940s. The 'million years' is an unsurprising jokey exaggeration. Another implied elongation is to be found, a little later, in the debate about whether they are waiting in the correct place on the correct day. They cannot remember if this place is the same as the one in which they waited yesterday: it is as though they had been away for weeks or months or even years. (The point is not that this never happens in real life, but that it doesn't normally happen in plays. In other words, it is unconventional.) Conversely, when Pozzo responds to Vladimir's outrage at his treatment of Lucky, asking him, 'What age are you, if it's not a rude question [?]' (pp. 27–8), Estragon ignores the plausible suggestions and answers 'Eleven'. This time the joke (which Beckett altered and eliminated in revision, having never thought it funny) involves a *compression* of time.

Indeed the most spectacular and memorable distortion of time in the play is a compression, one which happens twice, once in each Act:

> *The light suddenly fails. In a moment it is night. The moon rises at back, mounts in the sky, stands still, shedding a pale light on the scene.* (p. 52)

But this is the event Vladimir and Estragon have been waiting for all day (not counting the arrival of Godot), and such is their relief at its happening, they do not even remark on its suddenness. It is we who are puzzled by it.

The processes of nature in *Godot* seem bizarrely accelerated to create maximum perplexity, for at the opening of Act II the hitherto bare tree has leaves on it. The four or five leaves of the standard text (three in the revision) merely tease the men's (and our) comprehension, but the French tree, which is covered with leaves, seems almost to mock it. This is, after all, a stage direction tells us, only the next day. But performance knows nothing of stage directions, and when Vladimir prompts Estragon to remember 'yesterday' it seems half a lifetime away in another implied elongation of time:

VLADIMIR: And Pozzo and Lucky, have you forgotten them too?
ESTRAGON: Pozzo and Lucky?

VLADIMIR: He's forgotten everything!
ESTRAGON: I remember a lunatic who kicked the shins off me. Then he played the fool.
VLADIMIR: That was Lucky.
ESTRAGON: I remember that. But when was it?
VLADIMIR: And his keeper, do you not remember him?
ESTRAGON: He gave me a bone.
VLADIMIR: That was Pozzo.
ESTRAGON: And all that was yesterday, you say?

(p. 61)

Beckett's revised text of the play mines away at even Vladimir's memory – of the tree (alterations and additions are in square brackets):

ESTRAGON: Was it not there yesterday?
VLADIMIR: Yes, of course it was there. Do you not remember? We [all but] hanged ourselves from it. [(*Considers*.) Yes that's right, all -, but -, hanged -, ourselves from it.] But you wouldn't. Do you not remember?

(1993, p. 54)

After which hesitation, Estragon's 'You dreamt it' seems much more of a possibility, and Vladimir's 'Is it possible that you've forgotten already?' applies to himself too. For Estragon, himself a dreamer, the leaves on the tree are explained by Vladimir's delusions of memory:

ESTRAGON: It must be the Spring.
VLADIMIR: But in a single night!
ESTRAGON: I tell you we weren't here yesterday. Another of your nightmares.

(p. 66)

Making sense of the compression in time leaves them with the even more disturbing possibility that one may come to believe the things one dreams. The alternative (Estragon's alternative) is to assume the normative behaviour of nature, concluding that you were therefore elsewhere and that (Spring being general) 'yesterday' was some time ago – if indeed it is true that there were no leaves yesterday. We, the audience, of course stick with Vladimir.

It is worth pointing out that, in the midst of these disorientating exchanges, references to time which make its passage seem normal, and which are not afflicted by more-than-normal uncertainty, have a telling emotional effect. Long-term memory is the less problematic kind in this play. When night has fallen and the moon is up, Estragon harks back many years, and the effect is extraordinarily intimate:

> ESTRAGON: How long have we been together all the time now?
> VLADIMIR: I don't know. Fifty years perhaps.
> ESTRAGON: Do you remember the day I threw myself into the Rhône?
> VLADIMIR: We were grape-harvesting.
> ESTRAGON: You fished me out.
> VLADIMIR: That's all dead and buried.
> ESTRAGON: My clothes dried in the sun.
> VLADIMIR: There's no good harking back on that.
>
> (p. 53)

Before the fall of night, though, the mechanics of memory are profoundly troubled. The presence of the blind Pozzo in Act II further compromises the perception of time. His request to be told the time leads (in a passage cut from the revised text) to some comic complications. His elegy to his lost sight (also cut) – 'Wonderful! Wonderful, wonderful sight!' – sounds like an apostrophe to something long regretted. ('[H]e's thinking of the days when he was happy', notices Vladimir.) Pozzo declares, 'I woke up one fine day as blind as Fortune' but does not know which day or when. He rebuffs 'violently' the idea that the blind man is necessarily a seer (p. 86). He cannot see into the future and has no memory of the past: 'I don't remember having met anyone yesterday. But tomorrow I won't remember having met anyone today' (p. 88). This from the man who was so careful of his watch in the first act – the treasured heirloom of the Pozzos, '[a] genuine half-hunter [. . .] with deadbeat escapement!' (p. 46). Finally, under pressure from Vladimir's need to establish certainties, he delivers the most savage of the play's compressions of time:

> POZZO: (*suddenly furious*). Have you not done tormenting me with your accursed time! It's abominable! When! When! One day, is that not enough for you, one day like any other day, one day he went dumb, one day I went blind, one day we'll go deaf, one day we were born, one day we shall die, the same day, the same second, is that not enough for you? (*Calmer.*) They give birth astride of a grave, the light gleams an instant, then it's night once more. (p. 89)

He is a seer after all: the blind man's perspective reduces the whole of life to an insignificant instant. When, moments later, Vladimir takes up Pozzo's image, his version both elongates and compresses; to be precise, it *elongates* the *compression*, elaborating it to the point of grotesquerie:

> Astride of a grave and a difficult birth. Down in the hole, lingeringly, the grave-digger puts on the forceps. We have time to grow old. The air is full of our cries. (*He listens.*) But habit is a great deadener. (pp. 90–1)

Life is a birth into death, as in Pozzo's conception, but now it is lingering, lasting a 'normal' lifetime. Yet to subject the imaginative compression to imaginative elongation is decidedly *not* to arrive back at a conception that is anything like the normal perception.

For this is the effect of these dislocations and refigurings of time and memory. Our normal perception of the course of time is disturbed and thereby made strange, defamiliarized. This is not exactly because we are in the same position as the characters. Vladimir wants to remember; the others are mostly indifferent or, finally, hostile to the effort involved. Insofar as they are uncertain in Act II about what happened in Act I, we don't share this uncertainty: we remember well enough what happened before the interval. True, we might wonder if the boots on stage are indeed the ones Estragon left. What colour were they? What colour exactly are these? Why are they too big now, after being too small then? Still, we can say that all this tells us more about petulant, insentient Estragon than about the boots. But the tree: those leaves? Pozzo's sudden blindness; Lucky's sudden dumbness. And – we see it with our own eyes – the immediacy of nightfall and moonrise. We tell ourselves there is no problem: we are in the theatre; the characters are simultaneously on a country road and on stage. There is a tree there, and a stone. We see these. But offstage there is a corridor and there is a toilet 'on the left' (p. 35). It is a theatre, and we always knew that.

However if we engage with the play, the disturbance will not go away. As part of dramatic convention (which is what makes our audiencehood possible in the first place), we recognize the stage world as having similarities to our own, and we acknowledge the characters as being sufficiently like us to encourage sympathy and even identification. We allow for the fallibility of their memory. But the leaves on the tree and the moonrise fall outside the boundaries of recognition – or rather, the timescales involved do. The confidence of our recognition is disturbed and the framework of our understanding shifted. It is just not enough *like* nature. It seems that the compressions and elongations of time implied in the dialogue are not merely subjective impressions of experience in a 'normal' world (we can accept these) but have their 'objective' counterparts in the nature that the play gives us. Or, to put it another way, subjective and objective are no longer straightforwardly distinguished. The effect is that we have been invited to recognize as essentially our own a world which, with minimal alteration, suddenly turns strange. Far from dissociating ourselves from our original recognition, we strive to accommodate the strangeness. It is for this reason that we are closer to Vladimir and Estragon in Act II even than we were in Act I, because they are doing the same, and we can no longer reserve for ourselves a position of superior knowledge. Of course the terms of our understanding are different from theirs: where they live the confusion, ours is determined by our assent to dramatic convention. But these different terms don't qualify a superior knowledge. Indeed, insofar as we feel first Pozzo's, then

Vladimir's, image of the birth astride-of-a-grave to be a true perception, we trust and follow *them*. We feel now that they have access to insights that we can come by only *through* them. All this is an achievement not of philosophy or magic but of stagecraft – simple yet inspired.

Puzzles and difficulties in *Waiting for Godot*, then, are not unfortunate irritabilities that need to be dealt with before we get to grips with the play. Rather, they are an essential part of its effect on the audience. It remains to consider how these difficulties might relate to the chief thematic concerns of the play.

MEMORY AND SEQUENCE

We have already contemplated the comic scenario in which the faculty which is called upon to establish certainty only intensifies bafflement. This does not stop the characters resting the guarantees of their very being on memory, in a process which Steven Connor calls 'anticipated retrospect' (1988, p. 119). In his annoyance Pozzo reacts against this habit of Vladimir's when he exclaims: 'I don't remember having met anyone yesterday. But tomorrow I won't remember having met anyone today. So don't count on me to enlighten you' (p. 88). This mental operation – imagining tomorrow if or how one will remember today – also marks Vladimir's parting words to the Boy in Act II. In Act I, in answer to the Boy's 'What am I to say to Mr. Godot, sir?' he had replied: 'Tell him . . . (*he hesitates*) . . . tell him you saw us. (*Pause.*) You did see us, didn't you?' (p. 52). In Act II he makes the same request, but adds '*with sudden violence*': 'You're sure you saw me, you won't come and tell me tomorrow that you never saw me!' (p. 92). Not just witness, but the anticipated memory of witness is what matters.

So it is, too, when Vladimir takes stock of what has happened – what can be *said* to have happened – today, in his great speech immediately prior to the arrival of the Boy: 'Was I sleeping, while the others suffered? Am I sleeping now? Tomorrow, when I wake, or think I do, what shall I say of today?' (p. 90). His doubts about the state of his consciousness have become radical, hence the puzzlement about waking or sleeping. Under these circumstances, the memory of witness and the witness of memory chase each other round in a never-ending circle. Indeed recollection in this play can end up swallowing itself. In Act II, Vladimir and Estragon not only spend much of their time recollecting what happened in Act I; some of what they recollect is their own activity of recollecting. Estragon comes close to registering this: 'Yes, now I remember, yesterday evening we spent blathering about nothing in particular' (p. 66). Providing themselves, in fact, with the blather about which they can blather *this* evening.

This is not mere curious irony. For one thing, it should prompt us to remember Vladimir's song from the beginning of Act II, about a dog who comes into the kitchen, is beaten to death by the cook and is found by the other dogs, who bury the dead dog under a stone, telling the story of a dog who comes into the kitchen . . . (pp. 57–8). In its turn, Vladimir's song draws our attention to the importance of repetitive sequence – not just *in* the play but as a phenomenon that *encloses* the play. 'Off we go again', exclaims Estragon when the Boy enters, not in Act II but already in Act I (p. 49; it is Vladimir who has the same line in Act II). And when Pozzo and Lucky leave and Vladimir exclaims, 'How they've changed!' (p. 48), it is, oddly, in Act I rather than (or as well as) Act II. We know, and we can even anticipate if we don't know the play, that Act II will deliver a varied repetition of the pattern of Act I, but Estragon's reaction makes us acutely aware of something we had already inferred at the outset but had probably forgotten: that Act I is *already* a varied repetition of an action – a proto-Act, so to speak – that we haven't seen. And so on, back to no original term. There is no reason why the sequence shouldn't also stretch in the other direction, after Act II. In other words, the two acts of the play take their imagined place within a virtual sequence of waitings which has no reason to be anything other than infinite.

The Act II efforts at remembering make us conscious that, in their terrible void of waiting, the necessity of Vladimir and Estragon is for material to talk about, to blather with: 'Yes, now I remember, yesterday evening we spent blathering about nothing in particular'. In this sense there is a strange reversal of priority: for the men, Act I is important because it provides *material* for passing the time in Act II. Each act seizes on and recycles what went before in the form of remembered material. Or rather, it would, if we were given a larger part of the sequence. Each act would, we can fairly assume, feed on the previous one. So what is at stake here?

Vladimir and Estragon are revealed as having a radically different relation to the past from the one we normally expect of the individual in our culture. Here no linkage or continuity is assumed, let alone created, between more or less agreed stable quantities – a shared past, personal or cultural, and a shared present. Instead, an ever-dissolving present nourishes itself with memories of a past which is itself nearly impossible to access. *Presence* is the issue. As Steven Connor puts it:

> Vladimir and Estragon, stranded in the not-yet or intermission of waiting, poised between the past that they no longer inhabit and the future which cannot commence until the arrival of Godot, can never *be* fully in their present either. (1988, p. 120)

This, then, is how *Waiting for Godot* plays out what the young Beckett called 'the poisonous ingenuity of Time in the science of affliction' (1965a, p. 15). What is poisoned is a stable sense of individual presence; the affliction reaches down to the roots of being. In 1931, Beckett had already anticipated Vladimir's 'Tomorrow, [. . .] what shall I say of today?' in asserting that the 'permanent reality, if any', of the personality 'can only be apprehended as a retrospective hypothesis'. He continues:

> The individual is the seat of a constant process of decantation, decantation from the vessel containing the fluid of future time, sluggish, pale and monochrome, to the vessel containing the fluid of past time, agitated and multicoloured by the phenomena of its hours. (1965a, p. 15)

'Individual', we are reminded by this statement, is one of those negatives (*in*nocent; *in*dependent) which our culture holds as an enduring positive. For Beckett's individual here sounds nothing if not dividual. This radical questioning of individuality is directly relevant to the dominant conception of character and relationship, character-*in*-relationship, in *Waiting for Godot*, which we now move to consider.

CHAPTER 2

PSEUDOCOUPLES AND CHARACTER

In this chapter I shall examine the kinds of relation which exist between Vladimir and Estragon, and between Pozzo and Lucky. Before going on to discuss particulars of character in later chapters, I shall consider the implications of this relation for the conception of character as such.

'IT'S ALL SYMBIOSIS'

Of all Beckett's earlier writings, the one which is closest to *Godot* is not a play but a novel. In *Mercier and Camier* (written in 1946, but published in French only in 1970 and translated into English in 1974), an unnamed narrator recounts the wanderings and eventual parting of Mercier, a 'long hank' with a beard, and Camier, the 'little fat one' (1974, p. 48), through a recognizably Irish landscape. A large proportion of the narrative consists of dialogue. The reflexive principle is apparent in an early exchange between Mercier and Camier about two copulating dogs:

Don't look, said Mercier.
The sound is enough, said Camier.
True, said Mercier.
After a moment of silence Mercier said:
The dogs don't trouble you?
Why does he not withdraw? said Camier.
He cannot, said Mercier.
Why? said Camier.

One of nature's little gadgets, said Mercier, no doubt to make insemination double sure.

They begin astraddle, said Camier, and finish arsy-versy.

What would you? said Mercier. The ecstasy is past, they yearn to part, to go and piss against a post or eat a morsel of shit, but cannot. So they turn their backs on each other. You'd do as much, if you were they.

Delicacy would restrain me, said Camier.

And what would you do? said Mercier.

Feign regret, said Camier, that I could not renew such pleasure incontinent.

After a moment of silence Camier said:

Let us sit us down, I feel all sucked off.

(1974, pp. 11–12)

Grotesque couplings, natural or unnatural, are the order of the day: high rhetoric with slang, dog with bitch, French with English (in the odd literality of the translation: 'What would you?') and Mercier with Camier. The collocation has been painstakingly set up earlier, when the two men, still locked in a prolonged embrace following their rendezvous, seek refuge from the rain in a pagoda in a public garden:

Shadowy and abounding in nooks and crannies it was a friend to lovers also and to the aged of either sex. Into this refuge, at the same instant as our heroes, bounded a dog, followed shortly by a second. Mercier and Camier, irresolute, exchanged a look. They had not finished in each other's arms and yet felt awkward about resuming. The dogs for their part were already copulating, with the utmost naturalness. (1974, p. 9)

Even Mercier and Camier register the likeness between themselves and the dogs – hence, presumably, the awkwardness. Far from being downplayed, the sexual element of their embarrassment is pushed forward. The dogs are copulating, after all. Where they have finished but cannot part, the men have 'not finished' and are reluctant to part. Sexuality is generally more in evidence in *Mercier and Camier* than in *Godot*, but then in the

46

novel the men have the welcoming Helen ('There's my bed and there's the couch' (1974, p. 27)). To say that Vladimir and Estragon are like a married couple is a routine observation. Nevertheless it is still not clear what Estragon means when he remembers biblical illustrations of the Dead Sea: 'That's where we'll go, I used to say, that's where we'll go for our honeymoon' (p. 12). There is, one reflects, only one We in this play. The homo-erotic aspect of the coupling is not developed in the play, but that does not mean it is not there (see Boxall 2004).

The episode of the meeting in *Mercier and Camier* is a fictional definition of a particular sort of relationship – though 'relationship' is not quite the right word, implying as it normally does two parties who have a definite separate existence. For this is precisely what is at issue. When they are spoken of as falling, late in the novel, they are seen as 'two collapsing simultaneously, as one man, without preconcertation and in perfect interinde-pendency' (1974, p. 102). If they are reluctant to dump Mercier's raincoat, it is perhaps because it somehow represents them 'as one man':

Let it lie there, said Camier. Soon no trace of our bodies will subsist. Under the action of the sun it will shrivel, like dead leaf.

We could bury it, said Mercier.

Don't be mawkish, said Camier.

Otherwise someone will come and take it, said Mercier, some verminous brute.

What do we care? said Camier.

True, said Mercier, but we do.

(1974, p. 66)

The raincoat could be said to embody their oneness, just as their dialogue strongly implies 'the horrors of soliloquy' (1974, p. 78). Except that 'oneness' is precisely as inaccurate (*and* as accurate) as 'relationship'. If Mercier and Camier are not quite two (and therefore not two at all), they are not exactly one either. It is another of Beckett's narrative voices which supplies the best term for this state of being. In an inspired coinage the narrator of *The*

Unnamable refers to 'the pseudocouple Mercier-Camier' (1959, p. 299). *Pseudo* (Greek): false; *pseudein*, to lie. 'Pseudocouple' is ideally suggestive because it takes away 'couple' even as it gives it. Mercier and Camier are not, or not merely, interdependent but (as when falling) inter*in*dependent – *both* interdependent *and* independent yet not quite either of those. Like all portmanteau words, this is a verbal pseudocoupling. It registers effectively not just the tendency towards mutual reliance but the residual tensions of separateness.

Although the interindependence is not only verbal, in *Waiting for Godot* it is first of all verbal. This is a matter of style, certainly, but it is, to misquote William Empson, the style they learn from a refusal to despair. 'Silence is pouring into this play like water into a sinking ship' (qtd in Fletcher 2000, p. 52), Beckett himself once insisted. In Act II especially, the dialogue is shaped, as Lawrence Graver says, by a 'realization that to pass the time and ward off the silence, talk must be sustained for its own sake, and this late in the day, conversation means invention' (2004, p. 58):

ESTRAGON: In the meantime let us try and converse calmly, since we are incapable of keeping silent.
VLADIMIR: You're right, we're inexhaustible.
ESTRAGON: It's so we won't think.
VLADIMIR: We have that excuse.
ESTRAGON: It's so we won't hear.
VLADIMIR: We have our reasons.
ESTRAGON: All the dead voices.
VLADIMIR: They make a noise like wings.
ESTRAGON: Like leaves.
VLADIMIR: Like sand.
ESTRAGON: Like leaves.
   Silence.
VLADIMIR: They all speak together.
ESTRAGON: Each one to itself.
   Silence.
VLADIMIR: Rather they whisper.
ESTRAGON: They rustle.

VLADIMIR: They murmur.
ESTRAGON: They rustle.
  Silence.
VLADIMIR: What do they say?
ESTRAGON: They talk about their lives.
VLADIMIR: To have lived is not enough for them.
ESTRAGON: They have to talk about it.
VLADIMIR: To be dead is not enough for them.
ESTRAGON: It is not sufficient.
  Silence.
VLADIMIR: They make a noise like feathers.
ESTRAGON: Like leaves.
VLADIMIR: Like ashes.
ESTRAGON: Like leaves.
  Long silence.
VLADIMIR: Say something!
ESTRAGON: I'm trying.
  Long silence.
VLADIMIR: (*in anguish*). Say anything at all!
ESTRAGON: What do we do now?
VLADIMIR: Wait for Godot.
ESTRAGON: Ah!
  Silence.

(pp. 62–3)

In this duet-like passage, character is almost irrelevant. Estragon is uncharacteristically orotund at the start, but as they get going, Vladimir leads, as usual. It could be said that Estragon's repetitions at the end of units (before the silences) are typically clueless. Yet these are an essential part of a lyrical pattern. (The passage has even been extracted and reprinted in an anthology of modern Irish poetry.) It is in order to demonstrate this pattern – of echo, rhythm and varied repetition – that I have needed to quote at length. As James Mays has written about Vladimir and Estragon in general: 'It matters less that different tendencies of character can be distinguished, or that each occasionally acts out of such character as has been established, than that they are wedded like alternations of a pendulum' (1987, p. 160).

In any case, character distinctions would be a distraction from the essence of this passage. Speaking of their incapability of silence, they speak of generating words to drown out the dead voices. But the onomatopoeic quality of their own utterances ('rustle', 'murmur', 'ashes', 'leaves') ends up reproducing the dead voices, which are similarly obliged to talk. So the men talk of voices talking, talk to stop themselves hearing the voices talking, but end by echoing, even recreating, the voices they wish not to hear. A dog came in the kitchen. The silences (not now mere pauses) marked as stage directions are momentary floodings-in of that which they, and the dead voices, try to keep out. Thus the dialogue folds back on itself reflexively. It is as though invention, generating talk, cannot help but arrive at reflexivity.

Although character differences are scarcely relevant, the progression of the passage is essentially antiphonal: the talk could only be generated by the *two* of them held in the temporary unity of their pattern of words. The swing of the pendulum (to adopt James Mays' simile) is inevitable because of the gravity of their mutual need. For every dialogical tick there must be a tock:

> What do we do now?
> I don't know.
> Let's go.
> We can't.
> Why not?
> We're waiting for Godot.
> (*despairingly*). Ah!
>   (p. 48)

Character-distinction may be unimportant, but *two-ness* is essential. Comedy follows from this two-ness not being the same thing as harmony. For every embrace, there is a repulse; for every approach a retreat:

> ESTRAGON: Why will you never let me sleep?
> VLADIMIR: I felt lonely.
> ESTRAGON: I was dreaming I was happy.
> VLADIMIR: That passed the time.

ESTRAGON: I was dreaming that –
VLADIMIR: (*violently*). Don't tell me!
(pp. 89–90)

Neither can bear solitude. The best that can be said of it is that it produces Vladimir's dog song and the unique parenthetic moment towards the end of the play in which he confronts their situation in his monologue. 'What have I said?' (p. 91), he exclaims at the end of monologue: it is as though he had temporarily entered a different, uncontrolled, phase of consciousness. Alone, he has not been himself. After both episodes he moves '*feverishly*' (pp. 58, 91) about the stage, attempting to allay his panic at solitude. When, at the beginning of Act II, he attempts to greet Estragon, the response he receives encapsulates their mutual feelings in interaction: 'Don't touch me! Don't question me! Don't speak to me! Stay with me!' (p. 58). To call this line contradictory (as some critics have) is to misconstrue the nature of the relation between Vladimir and Estragon. Contradiction implies the possibility of choice for Estragon; this is not a matter of choice – of relation*ship* – but of a mutual necessity. 'Like a rubber band, they come together time after time' (qtd in McMillan and Fehsenfeld 1988, p. 140), said the actor Stefan Wigger, responding as Vladimir to Beckett's direction in Berlin in 1975. 'We can still part, if you think it would be better' (p. 53) suggests a wanly reasonable Vladimir at the end of Act I. It is (inevitably) Estragon's turn at the end of Act II: 'If we parted? That might be better for us' (p. 94). And Falstaff might be thin; Hamlet might be the man of action: all are conditions memorably imagined in their respective plays, but nonetheless ultimately unimaginable. Vladimir and Estragon, like 'the pseudocouple Mercier-Camier' mentioned in *The Unnamable*, have an essentially hyphenated existence.

Their need for one another, then, and their need for one another's words, is absolute. As Steven Connor observes of Beckett's work in general: 'the self is always bound to, because constituted by, its ineradicable relationship to others. The separative ego is in a condition of permanent crisis in Beckett, precisely because of the ethical impossibility of separation' (1992,

p. 104). Ethics manifests itself almost as biology. When in 1956 the first English Estragon, Peter Woodthorpe, asked what the play was all about, Beckett replied, 'it's all symbiosis' (qtd in Knowlson and Knowlson 2006, p. 124). Symbiosis is the clearest model for interindependence, though the usual dictionary definitions don't register the specificity of the case. In the definition we require, each of the participating members (the symbionts) of the pair (the symbiote) is dependent upon the other for its existence. Subjectively, though, this existence is no more than an impression, as Estragon ruefully observes: 'We always find something, eh Didi, to give us the impression we exist?' Vladimir's response, 'Yes yes, we're magicians' (p. 69), raises the possibility that the symbiotic existence is mere illusion – yet another kind of stage-show. The pantomime, the circus, the music hall, and now the magic show: their very existence implied to be a sleight of hand (and word). We, the audience sitting in the theatre, watching their play, take his point.

SYMBIOSIS AND POWER

There is of course another pseudocouple in the play, and their relation is of a very different nature. But where we approached the relation of Vladimir and Estragon by way of texts by Beckett which preceded *Godot*, the most helpful approach to that of Pozzo and Lucky is through Beckett's later work. In taking this retrospective view there is always the danger of suggesting the presence of a grand design in Beckett's *oeuvre*, as though Pozzo and Lucky were always meant to lead to these later aspects of their author's work. This would be a nice irony in itself, as Pozzo is always driving Lucky on the way somewhere (though that somewhere turns out to be merely 'On!', in other words, nowhere). However, the suggestion is no more misleading than the unavoidable implication that *Mercier and Camier* is largely of value because its pseudocouple prefigures Vladimir and Estragon. This linear model of literary development is ill-suited to the discussion of a text which has itself always been described as more circular than linear in its progression. In my Introduction I employed an alternative model of the progression of Beckett's work as a whole. Suggested by his own early image of the 'ideal core of the onion', this is an approach which sees his *oeuvre* as a gradual exfoliation or stripping away of external (technical) means. 'The artistic tendency', said the young Beckett, 'is not expansive, but a contraction' (1965a, p. 64). As I now turn to Pozzo and Lucky, I point to strikingly similar patterns of relation in later texts as revealing clearly, even starkly, in stripped-down form, the essential structure of their pseudocoupling. (The illumination could of course be said to work both ways.)

Where Vladimir and Estragon are evidently social equals, Pozzo and Lucky are just as evidently master and slave. And where the waiting men are figuratively 'ti-ed' (p. 20), the travellers are literally tied. As Richard Dutton suggests:

> The rope is a symbol of symbiosis, perhaps, as much as of submission, and they are as interdependent as Vladimir and Estragon, albeit in a different style. As 'friends', or at least equals, Vladimir and Estragon represent a horizontal axis; as master and servant / slave, Pozzo and Lucky represent a vertical one. (1986, p. 71)

For at least a part of Beckett's original French audience, the idea of the pseudocouple would have been implicit within the 'vertical' social relation. On one level this is shown within the play. In Act I we see the masterful Pozzo driving his carrier along to sell him at the fair, and terrorizing him at almost every turn. In Act II the situation is shockingly, comically, different: Pozzo still commands Lucky absolutely, but is now plainly entirely dependent upon the slave. The dumb carrier carefully places in the hand of the blind master the whip with which he will be brutally driven towards no destination in particular. 'I suppose he is Lucky to have no more expectations', remarked Beckett (qtd in Beckett 1966, p. lxiii). The play makes clear, as we shall see, that the Act II relation, far from being a reversal of the Act I relation, is a clarification of its essential nature.

A further dimension, however, is worth noting. Among Parisian intellectuals in the immediate post-war period, the ideas of the philosopher G. W. F. Hegel (1770–1831) were especially fashionable. Essential to Hegel's conception of history, as described in the *Phenomenology of Spirit* (1807), is the relation of master and slave. Angela Moorjani shows that Hegel was mediated to many French readers at this time by the Marxist philosopher and teacher Alexandre Kojève (1902–68). In this modified form ('Hegel-Kojève', as Moorjani calls it, appropriately suggesting yet another pseudocoupling), 'history begins with a fight to the death and perseveres in the dialectic relation between those who would risk their life for prestige and recognition and those who would not, aristocratic masters and bondsmen / slaves' (2003, p. 73). For ratification of his self-identity, the master requires recognition from one whom *he* recognizes as a genuine human being. He receives it from the slave, but does not acknowledge the slave as properly human. 'Hence', says Kojève, 'he is recognized by someone whom he does not recognize. And this is what is insufficient – what is tragic – in his situation' (1969, p. 19). This tragic irony Beckett characteristically turns to grotesque comedy with Pozzo and Lucky. For, as we shall see in a later chapter, Pozzo is both thoughtlessly arrogant and comically anxious about gaining recognition and approval from any potential audience apart from his own slave.

The nature of the linkage of Pozzo and Lucky is directly addressed in the passage in Act I following Lucky's kicking of Estragon when the latter filches the leftover chicken bones from Pozzo's picnic. Pozzo philosophizes about the 'tears of the world', claiming that they are 'a constant quantity. For each one who begins to weep, somewhere else another stops. The same is true of the laugh' (p. 33). The constant quantity idea seems to be behind his claim to look, despite his advanced years, like a young man compared to Lucky. He orders the carrier to take off his hat, and when he does so, '*long white hair falls about his face*'. When Pozzo then takes off *his* hat, he is revealed as being completely bald. Between these two moments comes his most intriguing bit of information. The 'beautiful things' he has been speaking, 'Beauty, grace, truth of the first water' – all these, he says, were taught him by Lucky. 'But for him all my thoughts, all my feelings, would have been of common things' (p. 33). This claim too seems to be governed by the idea of 'constant quantity'. It is as though they are not just interindependent but virtually inter-changeable, on a sliding scale of dominance-subservience or superiority-inferiority. Pozzo was born master, but (if we are to believe him) Lucky was once the tutor. Now everything of humane value (in Pozzo's notion of things) has been transferred, as unfailingly happens in teaching and learning, to Pozzo. In return, Lucky got all the hair. And as he demonstrates in Act I, he also kept the frantic remnants of his ability to think, the mech-anism for which is somehow vested in his hat. Pozzo commands Lucky's great Think for the entertainment of Vladimir and Estragon, but the master becomes increasingly dejected and frantic during its crazy course. Momentarily, the icon of suffering has become the wielder of power through performance.

It is the fluidity of this bizarre relation that we need to keep in mind, together with its manifestation of interindependence, as we glance briefly at the plays which followed *Godot*. Pairs of characters recognizable as pseudocouples figure in most of Beckett's plays, whether written for stage or radio. In the present context, however, those examples in which a relation of power is evident are the most relevant to our purpose. Questions of power are of course implicit in any pseudocoupling, but they are fun-damental in the Pozzo-Lucky type, as they are not within the Vladimir-Estragon type.

As he was writing it, Beckett thought of his next stage play, *Endgame* (1957), as 'more inhuman than *Godot*' (Harmon 1998, p. 11). This is largely because of its central character, Hamm, and the nature of his relation to his symbiont, Clov. Holed up in a sealed refuge in the wake of some unspecified catastrophe, the blind, wheelchair-bound Hamm is served by the crippled but ambulant Clov, perhaps his son, and tyrannizes his legless parents Nagg and Nell, who are both confined to ashbins. Even physi-cally, master and servant interlock and interdepend: Hamm cannot stand and Clov cannot sit: 'Every man his speciality' (1986, p. 97). Outside the refuge, they agree, is death; and their resources, material and mental, are fast running out, but they hes-itate to end their savage game of survival. Clov cannot leave, and Hamm cannot stop performing. He, just as surely as Pozzo, is essentially a performer. In his turn he bullies performance from

Clov and forcibly elicits audiencehood from his 'canned' father. Thus the mutual dependence of all these figures is viewed within the context of performance, where the seasoned tragedian and the attention-seeking child are revealed as aspects of the same pattern of necessity. The all-powerful performer needs his audience, yet he is at the same time, by virtue of that need, pathetically subservient to that audience. For this reason, the performative pseudocouple is intrinsically unstable, as issues of power are always implicit within it.

In *Happy Days* (1961) the family-scenario of the *Endgame*-pseudocouple gives way to a marital situation. In a desert landscape, the respectable, loquacious, middle-aged Winnie is progressively buried in sand – in Act I up to the waist, in Act II up to her neck. She too performs her 'day', in increasing desperation and with minimal dialogical help from her only companion, her husband Willie. They are a pseudocouple nonetheless. She is increasingly immobile but never stops talking; he is mobile (on all fours) but almost silent. His presence hardly registers at times, but he is vital to her as either dialogue partner or, failing that, audience. She is alternately pathetically grateful and witheringly contemptuous. Like Vladimir, she has a sense of being watched. An extra element is also apparent: a piercing bell which wakes her and keeps her awake, therefore prompting her to perform. She experiences the bell as a kind of violation.

In *Happy Days* the bell is situated outside the pseudocouple, but in *Play* (1963) the coercive mechanism is revealed as being an essential element of the coupling itself. That coupling now begins to take on an increasingly disturbing sexual charge. Three figures, an adulterous husband, a betrayed wife and the Other Woman, are trapped up to their necks in funerary urns, facing '*undeviatingly front throughout the play. Faces so lost to age and aspect as to seem almost part of urns*' (1986, p. 307). Their 'Hellish half-light' (1986, p. 312) is varied only when a single mobile spotlight glares in the face of each of them momentarily, extracting from them as it does so the triple-faceted narrative of the adultery. The tempo is rapid, the response to the light immediate, the voices toneless. At the end the play is repeated. For this eternal triangle their torment could continue eternally. But there are variations possible for the light – of tempo, of intensity – and these are important indicators, for, as Beckett insisted to his first English director, 'the inquirer (light) begins to emerge as no less a victim of his inquiry than they and as needing to be free, within narrow limits, literally to act the part, i.e. to vary if only slightly his speeds and intensities' (1983, p. 112). The light, a note indicates, 'must not be situated outside the ideal space (stage) occupied by its victims' (1986, p. 318). This is because the inquirer-light has now become a *part* of the pseudocouple. The coupling is not now among the characters on stage but *between* them (considered as a single unit) and the tormentor. However, for this very reason, the light, inhuman though it is, is also subject to the fluid power-relations of the pseudocouple, being thus 'no less a victim' than the enurned trio.

In *Play*, then, the inhuman torturer is itself figured as victim within the performative pseudocoupling. In the early 1960s Beckett had written a group of radio plays (*Words and Music*, *Cascando*, *Rough for Radio II*) in each of which a dominant figure, an 'Opener' or an 'Animator', imposes, sometimes by coercion, a creative obligation upon a servant or victim-figure. As the play progresses the apparently all-powerful director-figure is revealed to be mysteriously dependent upon the outcome of these creative 'sessions', and so upon the capabilities of his pathetic victim. The performative pseudocouple finds a further variation in *Not I* (1972), where Mouth, detached from any body, isolated and frantically pouring out its stream of words, is attended by a mysterious djellaba-clad Auditor. This figure, of indeterminate gender, facing towards Mouth, makes four periodic gestures of 'helpless compassion' (1986, p. 375) which nonetheless have the apparent effect only of prompting further speech. Compassionate though it is, the audience-figure can only generate performance, even with interventions which are designed to relieve the suffering of speech. The performative pseudocouple is thus trapped in this self-perpetuating round.

Ohio Impromptu (1981) reaches towards a benign resolution of the performative pseudocouple. A Reader and a Listener, as '*alike in appearance as possible*' (1986, p. 445), negotiate the delivery of a narrative – Reader reading, Listener regulating the reading by a system of knocks on the table at which they both sit. The narrative tells of separation from the loved one and ghostly reunification through the act of narration, 'the sad tale a last time told' (1986, p. 447). The nearly identical couple, differing only in function, narrate a resolution of two into one and in doing so seemingly terminate their own functions, their own differences. However, the last play, *What Where* (1983) appends a grim coda in reverting to a scenario of serial torture. A quasi-anonymous figure called Bam obliges Bem, Bom and Bim ('*as alike as possible. Same long grey gown. Same long grey hair*' (1986, p. 469)) to torture each other in turn, in order to extract a confession, first concerning 'what', then 'where', and then *where* 'where' was confessed. And so it could go on, in circular and eternally regressive fashion. Yet the torturer Bam is split: he is both on the scene speaking and a voice heard from the shadows downstage left. His voice rehearses and directs the sequence, controlling the light and announcing the seasonal round. It is a last essay in the dramatic articulation of the torturer-figure himself mysteriously obliged: Bam is simultaneously inside and outside the action, pseudocoupled with his victims, each of them in *his* turn both torturer and tortured in an endless round of transferred coercion and suffering.

Bam, Bem, Bim, Bom: the names bring us back nearly 40 years to Pozzo and Lucky. In the first edition of *En attendant Godot*, in the passage I quoted in my Introduction (p. 35 of *Waiting for Godot*: 'Worse than the pantomime' 'The circus' 'The music-hall'), Vladimir and Estragon compare Pozzo and Lucky to the 'Stalinist comedians', Bim and Bom. These, as Ruby Cohn explains, 'were Russian clowns [of the 1920s and 1930s] who wrapped criticism of the Soviet regime in a cloak of laughter' (2001, p. 258). They have, as she notes, been haunting Beckett's work since the mid-1930s, and they are usually associated with torture. In the novel *How It Is* (written, in French, as *Comment c'est*, in 1959–60), the names which reappear in *What Where* are attached to the 'imaginary brothers' (1964, p. 123) of the narrator who crawls through the mud, in the darkness. In particular Pim is instructed by the narrator through torture, and will pass the instruction on by similar means. Bom too is involved in the pattern. It is a world of sequential couplings and abandonments, rendered in unpunctuated 'versets'. The nature of the linkages, defined near the end of the novel, should by now be familiar:

> linked thus bodily together each one of us is at the same time Bom and Pim tormentor and tormented pedant and dunce wooer and wooed speechless and reafflicted with speech in the dark the mud (1964, p. 153)

With this brief survey of some Beckettian couplings after *Godot*, the *performative* nature of the pseudocouple becomes increasingly clear. It is this which brings about the shifting power relations between the savagely interindependent parties, and it is this that has been revealed by the theatrical exfoliations of Beckett's drama. These later plays give us a lens through which we can better scrutinize Pozzo and Lucky. When we move to examine this pair in more detail it is essentially as performers that we shall consider them.

SYMBIOSIS AND INDIVIDUALITY

Quite how central the conception of the pseudocouple is to the very texture of Beckett's imagination is suggested by the ubiquity of the self-consuming reflexive sequences we noticed in the previous chapter. ('A dog came in the kitchen'.) For these too, as we saw, are structures of interindependency. The centrality of the conception is also suggested by the imagery of Vladimir's speech: 'Astride of a grave and a difficult birth. Down in the hole, lingeringly, the grave-digger puts on the forceps. We have time to grow old. The air is full of our cries' (pp. 90–1). 'They give birth astride of a grave' ('à cheval sur une tombe', says the French (2006, p. 332) – literally, on horseback, in the saddle, over a grave – but here without stirrups): even the posture emphasises the split 'doubleness' of the single female body. In this radical compression, the grave-digger doubles as midwife; even his instrument is simultaneously single (as an object) yet (grammatically) plural. For 'lingeringly', the French has 'rêveusement' (2006, p. 338) – literally, 'dreamily', or 'as if in a dream' – glancing at that phase

59

of unconsciousness which is also a strange form of awareness, if not of consciousness. And the cries that fill the air are simultaneously those of the newborn and the dying. The whole image is a rendering of a state of suspension *between* states, an in-between-ness in which we are both both and neither. That our paraphrase is strained should reassure us that Beckett's explorations are in a territory that is hard, and sometimes even impossible, to access through language.

And yet language is vital to the characters – almost, indeed, their only resource. Pseudocoupling, as we have seen, is a matter of a certain style of dialogue: question and answer; statement and retort; feed and punch; tit for tat; tick for tock. In drama we normally assume that the characters enter and they speak the dialogue; they could remain silent, but they don't; then they exit. Yet everything we have seen so far about *Waiting for Godot* pushes against these fundamental assumptions. Characters who could remain silent are stable: they are individuals, pre-constituted (so to speak) and prepared to utter according to whether or not they choose. But the characters we have been considering are anything but that. 'Say something! . . . Say anything at all!' – this does not sound like a character who experiences himself independently of language, or indeed independently of the other to whom he addresses his plea. This is the basic truth about the structure of the pseudocouple which we have been examining in this chapter: the symbionts are interindependent – interreliant yet in tension, sometimes extreme tension – with each other. They exist, we could say, in a sphere suspended *between* individuality and mutual unity. Rather than pre-constituted individuals speaking dialogue, we have instead characters whose selves are constituted by the connection between them. 'There is', observes Richard Dutton, 'always a sense in which the dialogue is driven more by its own form and pattern, more by the need to preserve itself, than by any real attempt to communicate' (1986, p. 74). Under these circumstances, Vladimir and Estragon are more accurately thought of as the *effect* of their dialogue than its origin. As Peter Gidal insists: 'They speak it, it speaks them, no emanation other than the holding of the characters to the text's needs' (1987, p. 157). 'What is there to keep me here?' asks Clov in *Endgame*. 'The dialogue', retorts Hamm (1986, pp. 120–1). *Godot* is not so consistently or explicitly metatheatrical as *Endgame*, but Vladimir and Estragon, imprisoned 'in the midst of nothingness' (p. 81), know this too, and could say the same.

How, then, are we to approach characters about whom it can be said 'the text speaks them'? In addition to asking the usual questions about character, we stay alert to the manifestations of character as *performance*, to the impromptu improvised assumptions by the characters of roles and attitudes, and to the variety of language and gesture that these roles and attitudes bring with them. We notice, therefore, the ways in which characters embody disharmony and contradiction within their behaviours: the ways, that is, that these individuals are split, are dividual. These are the signs of self-construction. It is with these emphases in mind that we now move to consider the characters of the play, and the relationships among them, in greater detail.

CHAPTER 3

ALONE TOGETHER: VLADIMIR AND ESTRAGON

CLOWNS AND CHARACTER

Being a pseudocouple, Vladimir and Estragon may be said to be composed of the distinctions between them. The qualities have frequently been rehearsed. Vladimir is the thinker, Estragon the one preoccupied with the physical; Vladimir is the reasonable one, Estragon the dreamer; Vladimir is hopeful and positive; Estragon negative and despairing; Vladimir's breath stinks, Estragon's feet stink; Vladimir initiates, Estragon responds; Vladimir steers, Estragon (reluctantly) follows; Vladimir tends to mobility, Estragon to immobility. Vladimir restless, Estragon inert; Vladimir vertical, Estragon horizontal; Vladimir sky, Estragon earth; Vladimir hat, Estragon boots; Vladimir mind, Estragon body. And so on. Though not often complimentary, they are always complementary.

There is plenty of opportunity to overturn these basic distinctions, as every reader or spectator knows. Nonetheless, they are a necessary starting point. As director, Beckett used the distinctions further to define stage space within the set. This is from the rehearsal diary of his associate director, Walter Asmus, in Berlin, 1975:

> Beckett says that Estragon is on the ground, he belongs to the stone. Vladimir is light, he is oriented towards the sky. He belongs to the tree. Is the rehearsal stage the same size as this one? It is very important because of the distance between

stone and tree. This distance must be very nearly the same (McMillan and Fehsenfeld 1988, p. 137)

In the revised text, which largely derives from this production, the famous description of the set is augmented: '*A country road. A tree. A stone*' (1993, p. 9). Estragon's '*low mound*' (p. 9) has been promoted to the status of essential co-ordinate – both for stage space ('downstage well off-centre left' (1993, p. 89)) and for character – and an extra term has thereby been added to the list of distinctions: Estragon is mineral, Vladimir vegetable. The stone is 'grey, oblong, and, like the tree, inadequate for two' (1993, p. 89).

In Berlin, tall, thin Stefan Wigger (Vladimir) and short, plump Horst Bollmann (Estragon) were costumed according to their complementarity:

Vladimir is going to wear black and grey striped trousers which fit him, with a black jacket, which is too small for him; the jacket belonged originally to Estragon. Estragon, on the other hand, wears black trousers which fit him, with a striped jacket which is too big for him; it originally belonged to Vladimir. In this way, the differing physiques of the two actors [. . .] become part of a whole visual concept. (McMillan and Fehsenfeld 1988, p. 137)

For Act II, jackets and trousers were exchanged: the fits and misfits were complementary. The revised text records how the physical complementarity (not just of these two actors, but as a principle of gesture and movement) was used to underline what was already there in the dialogue. For example (the added directions are in square brackets):

VLADIMIR: [*(Looking up)*] Well? Shall we go?
ESTRAGON: [*(Looking down)*] Yes, let's go.
(*They do not move.* [*Silence.*])

(1993, p. 85)

The vast majority of the meticulous stage directions that form the bulk of the additions to the revised text derive from Beckett's notebooks for the Schiller-Theater production. As the editors of the revised text note: 'Beckett himself referred to the "balletic" element of the play and it is scarcely an exaggeration to say that the directions that are set out in the Schiller notebook resemble a choreography performed to the "music" of the text' (1993, p. xii). Such terms are always used when this production is discussed, and rightly so. In interview, Walter Asmus emphasizes the theatrical purpose of the precise blocking of moves: 'It was not that Beckett wanted them to move like ballet dancers. It was simply to express the exactitude and that there was a design in the blocking that had a meaning' (Oppenheim 1994, p. 44). Very often the exactitude was instrumental in bringing out a meaning, or at least an experience, which was essentially comic: the 'choreography' of the revised text is designed to bring out the physical comedy of the couple's routines. Reviewing the Schiller-Theater production, Martin Esslin noted how its 'light and irreverent touch' consistently drew attention to Beckett's 'deep indebtedness to popular entertainment, above all the silent cinema, the circus and the music hall' (1976, p. 98). Before turning to some more elaborate examples, let us begin by remarking a tiny adjustment of detail in the revised text, which can be thought of as epitomizing the comic, even clownish, emphasis.

In any production, the tree needs to be 'skeletally thin and ashen' (1993, p. 89) – whether with two down-curving branches (as Beckett apparently preferred) or three (as in Berlin). In Roger Blin's original French production, David Bradby reports, the tree 'was made by wrapping tissue paper that had been painted brown round a framework of wire coat-hangers twisted together. The spindly result was anchored in a piece of foam rubber' (2001, p. 55). So the idea that they could successfully hang themselves from it, even if they had a strong enough cord, is pleasantly ludicrous. But getting the best out of the comedy is a matter of timing. It is a matter of the difference between this:

ESTRAGON: Let's hang ourselves immediately!
VLADIMIR: From a bough? (*They go towards the tree.*) I
    wouldn't trust it.

(p. 17)

And this:

> ESTRAGON: Let's hang ourselves immediately!
> (*They go to the tree.*)
> VLADIMIR: From a bough? I wouldn't trust it.
> (1993, p. 16)

The revision is funnier. The shift from 'towards' to 'to' helps. In the standard text they are checking, so that Estragon's enthusiasm (about getting an erection from hanging himself) can't be thought unjustified. 'I wouldn't trust it' is clued-up, possibly even ironic. ('Don't be such a fool'.) But the revised text brings us much closer to the naïvety of the clown figure. They stand at the tree and contemplate the ruin of even this hope. 'I wouldn't trust it' now sounds like understated pessimism. ('We could have a go, I suppose'.) The hopes are more cleanly (silently) raised, and therefore more decisively let down (like the hanged man).

The important difference, though, is between *kinds* of funniness rather than degrees of it. The humour of the clown is much more apparent in the revised text generally. It is physicalized, coordinated, detailed, demanding a certain discipline and even virtuosity from the players – or perhaps just a knowledge of a particular idiom, a specific set of techniques:

> ESTRAGON: [(*Moving away left*)] That wasn't such a bad little canter.
> VLADIMIR: [(*Moving away right*)] Yes, but now we'll have to find something else.
> (*They take off their hats, concentrate.*)
> ESTRAGON: [(*Advancing towards centre*)] Let me see. Let me see.
> VLADIMIR: [(*Advancing towards centre*)] Let me see. Let me see.
> [(*They turn just before collision.*)]
> ESTRAGON: [(*Moving away left*)] Let me see. Let me see.
> VLADIMIR: [(*Moving away right*)] Let me see. Let me see.
> (*They [halt and] put on their hats.*)
> What was I saying, we could go on from there.

ESTRAGON: What were you saying when?
VLADIMIR: At the very beginning.
ESTRAGON: The beginning of WHAT?
VLADIMIR: This evening . . . I was saying . . . I was saying.
ESTRAGON: I'm not a historian.
(1993, p. 58 [Added directions are in square brackets.])

It is not just the characters but the playwright/director and his performers who are making something out of nothing here. This is either clowning or it is nothing. Thinking is physicalized and the two players are organized in the simplest of choreographies. It is as pure an instance as one can find in the play (the *revised* play) of what in Italian *commedia dell'arte* was referred to as a *lazzo*.

The revised text is not merely Beckett's 1975 rethink of his 1949 comic action. Most of the notes he sent Peter Hall after seeing the first English production in 1955 also point firmly in the direction of greater comic stylization. At the moment in Act II when Estragon, having gone offstage to 'meet Godot', returns terrified but refuses to escape via the auditorium, Vladimir '*contemplates auditorium*' and comments, 'Well, I can understand that' (p. 74). Beckett notes: 'Vladimir should inspect audience at much greater length before saying *Well I can understand that*. All this passage played too fast' (Harmon 1998, p. 4). The metatheatrical drollery needed underlining. The fact that it is a moment of terror for one of the characters is a secondary consideration. Immediately afterwards, in a stage image Beckett thought of as being like something out of a Western (see 1993, p. 159), the two men stand back to back on look-out, each '*scans horizon, screening his eyes with his hand*' (p. 74). Beckett insisted to Hall: 'Strict symmetry of position when watching out. [. . .] Burlesque peering from under eye-screening hands' (Harmon 1998, p. 4). Again the pointer is to a gesture from a comic stage tradition.

A further example of how the revised text elaborates physical movement, developing it towards the clownish, raises important questions about how the behaviour of Vladimir and Estragon is to be viewed. Later in Act II, Pozzo and Lucky enter and immediately fall, forming a cruciform heap ('*perpendicular across each other*' (1993, p. 70)). In an often-cited passage, Vladimir and Estragon debate the best course of action. As they do so, wondering whether or not to help the fallen pair, they establish a pattern of advance-and-retreat towards and away from the 'heap'. The editors note: 'With each move they approach a little nearer' (1993, p. 162). As they identify Lucky and contemplate revenge, the choreography ensures that the movement from concerted cowardice to euphemistic greed is perceived as clownish (consider especially '*pushing up their sleeves*'):

> ESTRAGON: And suppose we gave him a good beating, the two of us?
> VLADIMIR: You mean if we fell on him in his sleep?
> ESTRAGON: Yes.
> VLADIMIR: That seems a good idea all right.
> [(*They go closer to the heap, pushing up their sleeves.*)]
> But could we do it? Is he really asleep? (*Pause.*) No, [(*they retreat*)] the best would be to take advantage of Pozzo's calling for help –
> In anticipation of some tangible return.
> ESTRAGON: And suppose he –
>
> (1993, p. 72)

Morally speaking, it is the *switch* of plan which is clownish, largely because it is so predictable, working as it does through a general, and therefore recognizable, moral type rather than any realistic psychology: the coward's cowardice can only be overcome by his appetites. But then, suddenly, another switch – this one entirely unpredictable and making sense only because we know the prime value they place upon anything that can be made the occasion for talk:

> ESTRAGON: And suppose he –
> [(VLADIMIR *takes* ESTRAGON'*s arm, leading him in an anti-clockwise circle upstage around the heap.*)]
> VLADIMIR: Let us not waste our time in idle discourse! Let us do something, while we have the chance! It is not every day that we are needed. Not indeed that we personally are

needed. Others would meet the case equally well, if not better. [(*They halt at the top of the circle a little off-centre right.*)] To all mankind they were addressed, those cries for help still ringing in our ears! But at this place, at this moment of time, all mankind is us.

[(*Pause. They pose.*)]

[POZZO: Help!]

VLADIMIR: Whether we like it or not.

[(*They continue to circle downstage, halt just right of the stone.*)]

Let us make the most of it, before it is too late! Let us represent worthily for once the foul brood to which a cruel fate consigned us! What do you say?

(ESTRAGON [*pulls free and, tired, sits,*] *says nothing.*)

It is true that [. . .]

(1993, pp. 72–3)

Their circular march, the pose, and the displaced interjection of Pozzo (in the standard text the speech is unbroken (p. 79)): all these revisions go towards defining the broadest possible comic tone. Of course, this always was an idle discourse about the idleness of discourse, but the revisions ensure that the elevated linguistic register and the pompous delivery work precisely *against* dignity and moral weight.

Critical reactions to this episode are instructive. Certain critics, for example, are seduced by Vladimir's highly quotable rhetoric. Lois Gordon, for whom these are 'the most dramatic moments of the play' (2002, p. 166), tells us that Vladimir 'calls for both stoicism and generosity to others'; 'he affirms the imperative of going beyond one's meanest urges to altruistic action', 'rejects aggression toward both himself and others' and 'reconfirms the only viable life alternative: that they wait and accept their act of waiting [. . .] *as* their life' (2002, pp. 80–1). For Gordon, Vladimir is 'not unlike' Shakespeare's King Lear counselling his daughter on withdrawal from the world. *Godot* teaches us, she says, that 'stoicism and altruism may be unredemptive in terms of a responsive cosmic agency, but they offer moments of personal regeneration' (2002, p. 80) – like this one.

But the passage can be read for moral negatives as well as for moral affirmations. Here is Thomas Cousineau, who certainly identifies the passage as 'an inspirational burst of rhetorical puffery', but continues:

> Whatever sympathy [Vladimir and Estragon] evoke in us is contravened by their irritating egotism, which is less noticed because of Pozzo's more histrionic exhibition of that frailty but is nonetheless an important motive underlying their behaviour. Whether Godot is God or a wealthy landowner, they hope that he will save them, but the expectation of some form of salvation has only enfeebled them and led to their present state of paralysis. (1990, pp. 29–30)

It seems hard to chide the clown so sternly for the self-interestedness that makes him funny, that is so openly demonstrated – that, indeed, makes him what he is. Insofar as Vladimir and Estragon are clowns, we are likely to feel that they have no choice, or that what choices they make are entirely predictable, and not the appropriate subject of moral scrutiny. When a realistic character makes choices, we assess these choices and form a moral attitude towards the character. But the clown does what the clown does: his 'choices' are specifically designed to produce a certain response from the audience rather than to promote the development of a character within the boundaries of expectation which we refer to as 'consistency'.

'Insofar as Vladimir and Estragon are clowns. . . .' This, though, is the point. At certain moments in the play, including this one, they are indeed clownish. Hence the jarring effect of the comments of Cousineau and Gordon, quoted above. But at other moments in the play, Vladimir and Estragon appear as very different *kinds* of character. We have already considered such passages in previous chapters, and later we shall consider more. The characters may in those other passages still be situated within some recognizable pattern or style of performance, but it is very different from the clown-mode. This is not a matter of characters behaving differently from one moment to another (which can be readily accommodated within a realistic framework), nor of different *roles* being assumed by the characters (as though they were solid themselves and merely exchanging masks). It is a matter of figures who move from one *mode* of performance to another, sometimes without even giving notice.

Consider a compact example of this movement, from early in Act I. Vladimir, having fixed his mind on the two thieves who, according to the gospels, were crucified with Christ, makes an attempt to get round to them:

> VLADIMIR: Gogo.
> ESTRAGON: (*irritably*).What is it?
> VLADIMIR: Did you ever read the Bible?
> ESTRAGON: The Bible . . . (*He reflects.*) I must have taken a look at it.
> VLADIMIR: Do you remember the Gospels?
> ESTRAGON: I remember the maps of the Holy Land. Coloured they were. Very pretty. The Dead Sea was pale blue. The very look of it made me thirsty. That's where we'll go, I used to say, that's where we'll go for our honeymoon. We'll swim. We'll be happy.
> VLADIMIR: You should have been a poet.
> ESTRAGON: I was. (*Gesture towards his rags.*) Isn't that obvious?
> *Silence.*
>
> (pp. 11–12)

The oft-cited passage of which this is a part is quite properly thought of as the very model of the kind of writing which distinguishes *Godot* – that which combines religious or metaphysical questions with music-hall cross-talk. The direction 'Silence' is a recognition that what precedes it is a punchline, just as what precedes *that* is a feed. Yet the tone of Estragon's speech which provokes Vladimir's observation is not itself in any way comic. It moves us momentarily away from the cross-talk even as it prepares the joke. The memory hovers between naïvety and nostalgic self-awareness. Then he remembers envisaging happiness and introduces the puzzling reference to the projected honeymoon. Its surge of anticipated joy is plain to hear, even though this is, typically in this play, a *memory* of anticipation. This is no clown, or even cross-talker, at least for this moment. And then comes the rueful joke, which is a good one.

Those (I don't exclude myself) seeking information about the men normally fall upon this bit about Estragon's past. He has been a poet. Later in the act he quotes (and adapts) Percy Bysshe Shelley (p. 52). That at least fits. And yet. His acknowledgement of this calling works as the punchline for a joke. We can have no illusions about why it is there. That he refers to some lines of Shelley later is hardly conclusive evidence of his calling. And there is nothing else in the play that Estragon-as-poet helps to explain. It is a bit of pseudo-information, only there for the sake of the joke. It is there *because* of the joke-structure, and not the other way round. When Estragon recalls what the pictures of the Dead Sea (yes, of course, the *Dead* Sea) meant to him, this, we feel, is a man for a moment speaking words out of the texture of his lived experience. This is a *character*, in an uncomplicated sense. But when Estragon delivers the punchline of the joke we know that, as with any punchline, the structure of the gag is the determinant: the words are, so to speak, speaking *him*. This is, in Peter Gidal's words, 'the holding of the characters to the text's needs' (1987, p. 157).

Within the space of a line or two then, even as the cross-talk feed-and-punch structure reasserts itself, Estragon exists in two different characterological modes: he is both orthodox dramatic character, with affecting, natural-seeming hints of an enigmatic past, and smart comedian delivering a laugh-line which may or may not (it doesn't matter) consist of reliable information. He is both – or he is neither. Beckett's blending of serious and comic is indeed virtuosic, as has long been recognized. But it leaves us – deliberately – disconcerted by the very mode of existence of these characters.

The distinguished German theorist Wolfgang Iser clarifies the dilemma by stating it more broadly and focusing on the conditions of laughter. Iser argues that our tendency to read Vladimir and Estragon as clowns ends up imprisoning us in a contradiction when we try to make sense of the metaphysical or religious aspects of the play. Certain allusions lead us in the direction of a religious reading, only for the play to present a block:

> If these characters are waiting for God or some such all-pow-
> erful figure, if their identities are somehow connected with the
> thieves on the cross, then clearly we can no longer regard them
> as clowns. This means that we have erected a concept of the
> characters – admittedly with the guidance of the text – and are
> then forced to dismantle this concept as soon as we are made
> to relate the comic paradigms to the overall action. (1992,
> p. 58)

For Iser, our laughter at the clown is first of all superior, then cut off or stifled in the perplexity of being confronted with our own efforts at making sense. It is a moment-by-moment process: we form our idea of Vladimir and Estragon, then we are forced to dismantle and reform it according to a different model. And this happens again and again. Our close scrutiny of some character-istic moments in the play bears out the case Iser makes in more general terms. As often with Beckett, perplexity is the creative point.

CHARACTER AND PERFORMANCE-STYLE

How, then, are we to *take* these characters?

One answer – implicit in much of my discussion so far – is that we take them in the way any given production invites us to take them. It is clear, as we have seen, that Beckett always had in mind for his play a stylized form of performance. 'Producers don't seem to have any sense of form in movement', he complained to Charles Marowitz in 1962, 'the kind of form one finds in music, for instance where themes keep recurring' (qtd in McMillan and Fehsenfeld 1988, p. 16). Form in movement is what the revised text of *Godot* makes explicit. As McMillan and Fehsenfeld insist, 'even as he wrote *Godot* Beckett envisioned in some detail how it would appear in a final staging. [. . .] In Berlin he at last chose to assume the dual roles of author and director in order to give *Godot* the fully visualized stage performance inherent in his text from the beginning' (McMillan and Fehsenfeld 1988, pp. 135–6). It could be said, therefore, that the revised text (which derives largely from the Berlin production), with all its meticulous notation of movement and gesture, is rather an indication of performance *style* than a prescription for any production. 'Within the limits of a specified text', Beckett insisted to a sceptical Marowitz, 'the producer has plenty of scope for interpretation' (qtd in McMillan and Fehsenfeld 1988, p. 16).

If this were only a question of the interpretations of director and players, the matter would be considerably less problematic. It is, however, also – perhaps predominantly – a question of favoured or available performance styles, and these vary from country to country, from culture to culture. The production team, led by the director, must take decisions on performance options all the time, and those decisions are taken within the framework of local conditions – actors' skills, performance tradition, assumed audience reaction. Style is particularly problematic where comedy is concerned. We are made aware of this when we read the account given by Michael Rudman of his conversation with Beckett prior to the production of *Godot* staged by Rudman at the National Theatre, London, in 1987. Rudman gave his notes to his actors, concluding in this way:

> My biggest single worry is that on the one hand he wants it to be funny (I think he wants it to be *really* funny and I think he *really* wants it to be funny), but on the other hand he wants the movements stylized, maybe a little bit like mime. My worry is that the English audience won't find that kind of thing or that way of doing things funny. My worry is that the English audience (and I suspect most audiences, except possibly for the Germans) will find things funny that are rooted in character and, dare I say it, in time and place. Still I think we must try to give him what he wants. (Knowlson and Knowlson 2006, pp. 270–1)

In fact, worries similar to Rudman's were voiced even by Beckett's German actors. During the rehearsal of the Act II falls for all four characters, Stefan Wigger (Vladimir) reacted to

Beckett's insistence on the balletic nature of the action by asking, 'Does that mean that there is to be no naturalism whatsoever?' 'But how can one prevent the loss of the human element, how can one prevent it from becoming sterile?' 'Should it take on a dryness?' Beckett responded by demonstrating moves, by insisting that it 'has got to be done artificially, with beauty, like ballet. Otherwise everything becomes only an imitation, an imitation of reality. [. . .] It should become clear and transparent, not dry' (McMillan and Fehsenfeld 1988, p. 140). Jonathan Kalb testifies to the result: 'In description this type of activity sounds contrived, but in the theater it actually turns out to be strikingly natural' (1989, p. 33). And James Knowlson is reassuring: 'The degree of stylization that was involved in Beckett's famous 1975 Schiller production of *Waiting for Godot* has, I think, been greatly overestimated in the English-speaking world' (1992, p. 15).

Nonetheless the anxieties remain, at least in the theatre. We can see Michael Rudman's worries at work, not in his production but in the 2005 one by Peter Hall (who had directed the first British production 50 years previously). Jonathan Croall observed Hall working with James Laurenson (Vladimir) and Alan Dobie (Estragon) on the moment, just after they agree that they've lost their 'rights', where they *remain motionless, arms dangling, heads sunk, sagging at the knees*' (p. 19). What the stage direction calls for is plainly, in Rudman's words, 'a little bit like mime':

> Peter continues to make small adjustments. 'I know Sam says you both have your arms dangling here during the silence', he tells them, 'but what you did belongs to another convention, it didn't contain the emotion, it seemed empty and contrived'. Alan suggests a different, less symmetrical stance, which overcomes the problem. (Croall 2005, p. 92)

'Containing the emotion' would seem to mean locating it within the image in such a way as to attract sympathetic identification from the spectator for the characters. They should not seem, as in this case they might, like marionettes whose strings have been cut. That would seem 'empty and contrived'. The response, in other words, would be, to use Rudman's phrase, rooted in *character* – where character means not the partial representative of a clownish pseudocouple but a substantial autonomous individual with recognizable psychological needs and desires.

The character-centred approach which Hall favours – the approach Anglo-American theatre has always favoured – is amply suggested by the way in which he distinguishes between the two characters: 'Estragon's function is not to change [. . .] but Vladimir goes on a terrible journey' (qtd in Croall 2005, p. 93). Split the pseudocouple and Vladimir – the thinker, the inquirer, the restless one – naturally becomes the more interesting character, with Estragon demoted to foil. Did not Beckett himself call Vladimir 'the spirit of the play' (Harmon 1998, p. 6)? In the terms used by Hall, perceived *change* of attitude is of primary importance. Role-as-journey has become the standard model within Anglo-American acting – and with justification, for it well suggests the essential linearity, together with the inevitable loops, reversals, aberrancies, recoveries and rediscoveries, of the dominant conception of the developing individual self. Characters are interesting, we feel, because they have the capacity to *change*. Now it would of course be wrong to assume that Hall or his actors merely carry around these assumptions and unthinkingly apply them to *Godot*: a director has ways of talking to actors which are, thankfully, far from the formulations of literary criticism. And we have already seen enough of Vladimir and Estragon to know that the character-led view is far from simply wrong. Nonetheless the dissonance, potential or actual, of performance styles is plainly there: stylized on the one side; character-centred on the other. It seems like a divide rather than a spectrum. The distinction I made near the beginning of this book between pattern and character is one that I have examined throughout in its several forms, but here it manifests itself as a genuine practical problem.

THE LAUGH AND THE TEAR

It seems that stylized and character-centred approaches can be integrated within particular productions. In his study of acting style in Beckett's drama, Jonathan Kalb praises Beckett's Berlin production, with the author-director's emphasis on stylization, for its ability 'to reconcile authentic realism with authentic artificiality' (1989, p. 32). It shows clearly, he says, 'that the two realms of meaning, presentational and representational, can be blended into a consistent atmosphere of ambiguity without the actors having to make constant shifts back and forth between them' (1989, p. 35). Kalb remarks on the success of Stefan Wigger (Vladimir) and Horst Bollmann (Estragon):

> The effect of their clownish appearance is to eliminate the possibility of spectators imagining real-life histories for them [. . .] and to call attention to their complementary senses of humour: one responds to the other's jokes so quickly and cleverly that it sometimes appears as if they have access to a common mind. (1989, p. 33)

This is as we should expect: by denying the audience the imaginative opportunity to wonder about the characters as individuals – their 'back-stories' and complex motivation – director and actors create the relationship of the pseudocouple. Surface rather than depth. As Charles R. Lyons says, the 'lack of detailed information about Vladimir and Estragon does not suggest a rich inner life that Beckett refuses to objectify. These characters are no more psychologically complex than they appear to be' (1983, p. 17). It all fits with Beckett's well-attested antipathy to motive-hunting – as when Sir Ralph Richardson 'wanted the low-down on Pozzo, his home address and curriculum vitae, and seemed to make the forthcoming of this and similar information the condition of his condescending to illustrate the part of Vladimir' (qtd in Knowlson 1996, p. 412). And so, as Michael Goldman states, 'it is clear [. . .] that Beckett rejects any performance mode that invites the audience in', so that 'there can be no cozy sharing of a human essence' (1986, p. 76).

All this is in danger of suggesting that the combination of character and pattern, clowning and metaphysics, results in coolness, that the price of clarity of outline is emotional distance, and that the audience is carefully positioned so as to be beyond the range

of emotional affect. I shall end this chapter by testing this suggestion against the last few pages of the play, for we find there a
potent collocation of the elements I have identified as not only distinct, but problematic in their interaction. Quite how they work to
position the audience is worthy of sustained scrutiny. Above all it
is the *tone* of the dialogue and action that we need to examine.

No sooner is Pozzo up after his entrance-fall than he wants to
be off. It is quite unlike Act I, when he had to admit, 'I don't seem
to be able . . . (*long hesitation*) . . . to depart' (p. 47). The revised
text goes some way to facilitating his exit by cutting a whole page
of mostly comic dialogue as Vladimir and Estragon hold him up
between them – like caryatids (as Estragon points out) or even
(we can speculate) the two thieves. Now Pozzo affirms his blindness, briefly laments his loss of 'wonderful sight' (p. 85) and
responds with irritation to queries about when he lost it. The dissonance of tones is perceptible:

> POZZO: (*violently*). Don't question me! The blind have no
> notion of time. The things of time are hidden from them
> too.
> VLADIMIR: Well just fancy that! I could have sworn it was
> just the opposite.
>
> (p. 86)

Even as he rejects the role of blind seer, Pozzo's tone has an ele-
vation that would not be out of place in tragedy. Vladimir's ironic
rejoinder, on the other hand, is a comic retort.

Two more excisions in the revised text keep the focus on Pozzo
as he, the ruined master, orders Vladimir and Estragon to find
Lucky ('Where is my menial?'). When Estragon dallies, an
exchange gives the opportunity for a surprise joke – the familiar
reprise turning up in unfamiliar form:

> POZZO: What is he waiting for?
> VLADIMIR: What are you waiting for?
> ESTRAGON: I'm waiting for Godot.
>
> (p. 87)

It's a good one, but the direction '*silence*' afterwards (not '*pause*') implies that laughter by now is weary, if not empty. (Walter Asmus reports that, in Berlin, Beckett wanted 'to avoid a superficial comic effect at this point' (McMillan and Fehsenfeld 1988, p. 146).) Pozzo responds to Estragon's cluelessness about how to get Lucky up by busily offering helpful practical advice on how best to coerce and brutalize the slave: 'he should give him a taste of his boot, in the face and the privates as far as possible' (p. 87). Of course this is well within the range of behaviour we expect of Pozzo, but when Vladimir encourages his friend to take revenge for Lucky's Act I kick, reassuring and advising on prior measures, we might be more troubled. We are invited to respond to Vladimir as he himself responded to the treatment of Lucky in Act I: 'To treat a man [. . .] . . . like that . . . I think that . . . no . . . a human being . . . no . . . it's a scandal!' (p. 27). Yet we also know by now that this is a comic set-up, another routine: the wary coward Estragon egged on and wisely counselled by solicitous Vladimir. Characteristically, the revised text choreographs the moment for physical comedy:

> (ESTRAGON *goes to Lucky*.)
> ESTRAGON: Don't take your eyes off me.
> (*He raises his foot to kick him*.)
> VLADIMIR: (*Halting* ESTRAGON*'s kick*) Make sure he's alive before you start. No point in exerting yourself if he's dead.
> ESTRAGON: (*Bending over* LUCKY) He's breathing.
> VLADIMIR: Then let him have it.
>
> (1993, p. 79)

And then the comic pay-off. Again the revised text carefully calibrates the humour. Where the standard text has Estragon kicking Lucky with '*sudden fury*', '*hurling abuse at him as he does so*' (p. 88), the revision has only, 'ESTRAGON *kicks* LUCKY, *hurts foot, hobbles limping and groaning to the stone*' (1993, p. 79). The suggestion is that this is now a cleanly and swiftly executed *lazzo* – a moment of violence more clearly signalled as comic because it is delivered as the last move in the structure of the visual gag. Estragon's complaint against Lucky as he limps off completes the comic reversal of attitude: 'Oh the brute!' (p. 88). Your body has hurt my foot: how dare you!

The revision makes no essential difference to our disturbance at this moment. This is because that disturbance is not primarily moral (good characters represented as doing bad things) but rather concerned with different modes of performance. Violence is rendered within a comic frame of perception, the routine or *lazzo*, and this frame of perception itself jars, as we have already seen, and will shortly see again, against non-comic modes or frames of perception. It is this jarring that disturbs us rather than the simpler moral contradiction of sympathetic Vladimir and Estragon planning and executing violence on prone and helpless Lucky. The disturbance, then, is structural, and categorical, rather than simply moral.

As Estragon falls asleep, Vladimir resumes his questioning of Pozzo. Curious he certainly is, and as ever needing to gather information the better to locate himself, in time especially. But more than this he wants to keep Pozzo *there*. The revised text underlines the point by adding the direction '*[h]olds him back by the arm*'; then in the ensuing dialogue he '*halts*' Pozzo and Lucky on three separate lines (1993, p. 80). The physical gesture gives a clearer idea of Vladimir's desperation. 'Don't go yet!' (p. 89) he pleads. For the blind Pozzo he gives a commentary on Lucky's actions. He seizes on the confirmations of Pozzo's and Lucky's identities (we don't notice that these haven't come before) and tries to extract confirmation of yesterday's events. Pozzo's inability (or disinclination) to provide it makes the events seem a long time ago – it is an elongation of the kind we noted in Chapter 1: 'You were bringing him to the fair to sell him. You spoke to us. He danced. He thought. You had your sight'. 'As you please', replies Pozzo (p. 88).

A dialogue insertion in the revised text (here in square brackets) gives us a Vladimir who is not just desperate but momentarily contemplative:

VLADIMIR: Where do you go from here?
[POZZO: No concern of mine.

VLADIMIR: How changed you are.]
POZZO: On.

(1993, p. 80)

'How changed you are' echoes his 'How they've changed!' after
the Act I exit of Pozzo and Lucky (p. 48). Here, though, the tone
is quite different. It is perhaps not sentimental to hear in it a note
of pity for the master whose lordly unconcern has its literal truth
in his impotence. At any rate, Vladimir's line prepares us to
receive two items of information, carefully held in reserve by
the playwright, which invite a perception of something which
approaches tragic irony. First this:

VLADIMIR: What is there in the bag?
POZZO: Sand. (*He jerks the rope.*) On!

Then this:

VLADIMIR: (*Halting them*) Before you go tell him to sing!
POZZO: Who?
VLADIMIR: Lucky.
POZZO: To sing?
VLADIMIR: Yes. Or to think. Or to recite.
POZZO: But he's dumb.
VLADIMIR: Dumb!
POZZO: Dumb. He can't even groan.

(1993, pp. 80–1)

The rhythms are those of the comic cross-talk, but the image
composed, with ferocious economy, is an icon of futility: the
dumb slave, laden with sand, leading the blind master nowhere
on. It is hard not to think, as other critics have, of Gloucester and
Poor Tom in that other play which inextricably combines the
comic with the tragic to frequently grotesque effect, *King Lear*:
''Tis the time's plague when madmen lead the blind' (IV.i.47).
Bert O. States, for whom Pozzo is the play's 'tragic relief' (1978,
p. 62), sums up this aspect: 'All told, what we have in the Pozzo /
Lucky plot is [. . .] tragedy's radical sequence reduced to a

remnant, to a before-after advertisement for the world's power to get even (and then some), and inserted into the continuum of a vaudeville routine' (1978, p. 65).

Pozzo is not just plagued by time but also by Vladimir's questions about it. I have already quoted (in Chapter 1) the resulting outburst ('*suddenly furious*') for its extraordinary imaginative compression of time. In our present context it appears as the climax of the play's tragic aspect – if it may be said to have one that is genuinely separable from the comic aspect. (Tragicomedy is yet another pseudocouple.) 'What is perhaps so stunning about the speech', States comments, 'is that one has the sense of a violent rent in the play's tragicomic veil through which we suddenly see what has been behind it all along' (1978, p. 66). We do indeed have here, with '[t]hey give birth astride of a grave', 'the sudden enlargement of [. . .] vision' (1968, p. 522) in the face of death which W. B. Yeats remarked in Shakespeare's tragic figures. Yet Vladimir's adoption of the same image just a few moments later should give us pause.

Tragedy is a world of singularities, of things that happen, catastrophically, once and uniquely, and of the unique individual – noble or not – who responds as death overtakes him or her. *Godot*, on the other hand, is a world of doublings and repetitions, of sequences which trip up singularities and compromise the dignity of the unique event, of interindependence rather than individuality, of impure couplings rather than pure essences. It is not a purely comic world, any more than it is purely anything else, but it is one in which the grand gesture is never immune from erosion. So it is with Pozzo's great speech, for the logic of sequence works here too. After Vladimir's recomposition, the authority of the speech is less than it was before, its claim to absolute truth compromised. Pozzo's image comes from one who is 'calmer' after his outburst. As usual in this play, 'cawm', as the English say (p. 16), is a good thing – or at least a better thing than the alternative. Composure and composition: he is composed; it is composed. Vladimir's version almost acknowledges its own composition – acknowledges, that is, that it is a *re*handling of a prior text – in the pauses enforced by the stops and commas: 'Astride of a grave and a difficult birth. Down in the hole, lingeringly, the grave-digger puts on the forceps. We have time to grow old. The air is full of our cries'.

And just as the varied repetition of Pozzo's image has created a sequence, the speech then acknowledges the idea of sequence: 'But habit is a great deadener. (*He looks again at Estragon.*) At me too someone is looking, of me too someone is saying, he is sleeping, he knows nothing, let him sleep on' (pp. 90–1). Tragic insight has been endowed with a grotesque element (the grave-digger equipped with forceps) and inducted into a hall of mutually reflecting mirrors.

Reverting to the passage between the two speeches, we get a strong sense of what produces Vladimir's one. His 'mimic' at the offstage fall of the disappearing Pozzo and Lucky re-establishes the tone of physical comedy, and then when Vladimir wakes the sleeping Estragon, the apologetic pathos of his explanation for doing so, 'I felt lonely', gives way to the violence of his refusal to hear his friend's dream. The tone of frustration and anxiety can hardly be contained within the cross-talk format, which is here disordered to the extent that the familiar refrain-exchange about waiting for Godot now turns into a broken-off mini-monologue for Estragon: 'Let's go. We can't. Ah!' (p. 90). Vladimir interrogates the idea of Pozzo's blindness – in the revised text speculating hard: 'Would one truly blind say he had no notion of time?' (1993, p. 81). When he concludes, 'It seemed to me he saw us', we know what is behind the enquiry. After telling his friend that he (Vladimir) must have dreamt that Pozzo could see, Estragon the dreamer is the one who voices Vladimir's anxiety – as though reading from their common mind:

> ESTRAGON: Are you sure it wasn't him?
> VLADIMIR: Who?
> ESTRAGON: Godot.
> VLADIMIR: But who?
> ESTRAGON: Pozzo.
> VLADIMIR: Not at all! (*Less sure.*) Not at all! (*Still less sure.*) Not at all!
>
> (p. 90)

The dribble of certainty turns into a haemorrhage before our very eyes and ears: a simple routine centring on a potential confusion of similar names, a routine which could have gone anywhere, has been positioned in the play to give it maximum effect. The comic pattern is obvious, but the tragic screw is turned. In this play where remembering is so effortful, some things are never really forgotten. They enter, as it were, into the memory of the play, then return later. We have barely moved on, it seems, from the first entrance of Pozzo in Act I:

ESTRAGON: (*undertone*). Is that him?
VLADIMIR: Who?
ESTRAGON: (*trying to remember the name*). Er . . .
VLADIMIR: Godot?
ESTRAGON: Yes.
POZZO: I present myself: Pozzo.
VLADIMIR (*to Estragon*). Not at all!
ESTRAGON: He said Godot.
VLADIMIR: Not at all!

(p. 22)

In Act II it is the same anxiety manifested in the same form: the similarity of the two names. But Vladimir's morale is now crushed. As Estragon complains about his feet again and resumes the old struggle with his boot, Vladimir declares, 'I don't know what to think any more' (p. 90). The word 'psychology' is surely unavoidable here, for us as for any actor of the role. This – the state that draws from him, the thinker, that admission – is the necessary psychological condition for his monologue. He has been dispossessed of all certainty, even the illusion of it. The monologue must be, as it does indeed turn out to be, an attempt to reconstruct from nothing.

As we saw in Chapter 1, Vladimir's monologue proceeds by a strategy of anticipated retrospection: 'Tomorrow, when I wake, or think I do, what shall I say of today?' (p. 90). It is fitting, then, that its final line should cause us to reconsider what we have heard in a slightly different perspective. After looking again at Estragon and evoking the image of serial observers, each one (it is implied) a dreamer, imagining he is awake, watching the dreamer who imagines he is awake, Vladimir declares, 'I can't go on!' Then, after a pause, he asks himself, 'What have I said?' (p. 91). The detailed blocking in the revised text gives a valuable confirmation of what is going on here. There is no look at Estragon, but a glance *'away upstage right'* for 'At me too . . .'; then *'he looks front'* at 'of me too someone is saying'. At the pause before 'I can't go on!' *'He goes silently upstage left, stands brooding'*, then before 'What have I said?' *'He looks back front to where he stood before'* (1993, p. 82). He moves away, therefore, from his original position, in order to look back at it. It is as though, we are to feel, the whole monologue has been delivered out of another sphere of awareness. For a moment he has stepped aside, alive, from the 'great deadener', habit, perceiving life as a dream-troubled sleep. Then he looks back to that place of realization into which he had stepped. No sooner has he done this than habit kicks in again with the arrival of the Boy: this is the weight of Vladimir's 'Off we go again' (p. 91). Bert O. States sums up the case:

> Vladimir, like Pozzo, stands outside himself, at a cross-road, a consciousness momentarily detached from the 'habit' of the body, represented by the sleeping Estragon who serves, at this moment, as a condensation of the whole principle of waiting. (1978, p. 110)

The directions in the revised text serve to make his standing 'outside himself' literal; but then the image of the difficult birth asks us to wonder if he ever had a finished self to stand outside. His desperation that the Boy will testify, both to Godot and to Vladimir himself, to having *seen* him expresses precisely this sense of the absence of a self. He must be *witnessed*.

I have discussed Vladimir's dialogue with the Boy, in Chapter 1. We considered there the effect of the addition of the colour red to the speculation about Godot's beard. Apart from this detail, the dialogue remains the same as in the standard text. However, the visual character of the Boy's entrance, exit and presence are quite different, even though the revised text only hints at this. The hint is in the revision of his exit: in both acts the *'exit running'* (p. 92) of the standard text is replaced by *'The* BOY *exits calmly backwards'* (1993, p. 83). The editors note that 'Beckett ensured that the wings at each side of the raked stage at the Schiller-Theater were shrouded in shadow'; this 'reinforced the sense of a scene that comes out of and returns to darkness' (1993, p. 90). The Boy too comes out of and returns to darkness, and with a form of movement which is much nearer to ritual than in the standard text. The editors further report that in the San Quentin Drama Workshop production Beckett commented that the voice of the Boy 'should appear to come from another world' (1993, p. 141). (The Act I instruction to deliver the message *'in a rush'* (p. 50) is cut from the revised text.) His exit even seems mysteriously to cue the rapid fall of night and the inscrutable moonrise. These details amount, I think, to a further complication of Vladimir's sense of being. What kind of world does he now perceive himself to be in? It has turned strange. Noting that the 'revision here differs markedly in tone and visual effect from the published texts', the editors comment:

> Vladimir no longer seems to threaten the Boy, causing him to turn and run in flight. Instead of an unstructured violence of conflict and fear, his calm exit backwards emphasizes the pattern of a world that returns quietly to its starting point. The Boy's calm, deliberate disappearance into the darkness from which he was first heard to speak also momentarily directs attention to that darkness and allows contemplation of what it might contain. (1993, p. 143)

The revision gives (and in performance it gave) a far stronger sense of immanent *design* than anything conveyed in the standard text. The unforthcoming ritual messenger, the brief catechism, the surrounding shadow, the sudden fall of night and rise of moon, and the whole substantially a repetition of a sequence that has occurred before, and will occur again: pattern is surely here working to intimate some larger presence.

And of course, just as surely, this is never confirmed. How can it be? Yet how far we are here from the conventional territory of comedy. Then Estragon wakes and the familiar pattern of exchange reasserts itself, though with a changed tone:

ESTRAGON: What's wrong with you?
VLADIMIR: Nothing.
ESTRAGON: I'm going.
VLADIMIR: So am I.
ESTRAGON: Was I long asleep?
VLADIMIR: I don't know.
   Silence.
ESTRAGON: Where shall we go?
VLADIMIR: Not far.
ESTRAGON: Oh yes, let's go far away from here.
VLADIMIR: We can't.
ESTRAGON: Why not?
VLADIMIR: We have to come back tomorrow.
ESTRAGON: What for?
VLADIMIR: To wait for Godot.
ESTRAGON: Ah!

(pp. 92–3)

Estragon's next line, 'He didn't come?' is actually very funny, when one thinks about it. But we don't laugh. For us, as for them, night is a rather different phase of experience. Earlier there was the innocent stage direction, '*Estragon wakes, takes off his boots*' (p. 92). Just like that! His struggle with his one boot opens the play; in the moonlight it seems that two come off quite readily (and now he thinks they are too big!). The moonlight even affects the way one speaks: in the revised text Estragon's enquiry about Godot, 'And if we dropped him?' (1993, p. 84) is whispered. And in his notes to Peter Hall in 1955, Beckett writes that from the exit of the Boy 'to curtain *dead numb tone* for Vladimir' (Harmon 1998, p. 5, Beckett's emphasis). The injunction is repeated specifically for 'Everything's dead but the tree' (p. 93), a generalization which, we are invited to feel, includes the men themselves. The dead numbness is implicit in the writing. An exchange about the tree echoes a much livelier one near the beginning of the play (p. 14):

ESTRAGON: What is it?
VLADIMIR: It's the tree.

ESTRAGON: Yes, but what kind?
VLADIMIR: I don't know. A willow.

(p. 93)

'Let's go', adds the revised text, as 'VLADIMIR *takes* ESTRAGON's *hand and they go to the tree, halting with* VLADIMIR *to the right and* ESTRAGON *to the left of it'* (1993, p. 84). It is the last visual allusion to the two thieves crucified with Christ, and it prepares for the final contemplation of suicide. As in Act I, Vladimir is the one who urges Estragon to go and Estragon detains him with thoughts of hanging. In addition, the revised text directs a pattern of hand-taking and subsequent release which makes them seem closer than they have seemed hitherto.

The last suicide plan is the most daring of Beckett's comic sallies, coming as it does amidst the dead numbness of the scene. Literally daring, for it dares us to laugh at falling trousers, a move so quintessentially clownish that it can hardly fail to present itself for scrutiny within (so to speak) inverted commas. It is the very sign of innocent clowning, appearing in the very midst of their hopelessness and at the very end of our experience of the play:

ESTRAGON: Wait, there's my belt.
VLADIMIR: It's too short.
ESTRAGON: You could hang on to my legs.
VLADIMIR: And who'd hang on to mine?
ESTRAGON: True.
VLADIMIR: Show all the same. (*Estragon loosens the cord that holds up his trousers which, much too big for him, fall about his ankles. They look at the cord.*)

(p. 93)

When the first French Estragon, Pierre Latour, apparently for reasons of personal dignity, compromised on the fall of his trousers, Beckett's partner Suzanne reported it to him, and he wrote to the director Roger Blin. The letter constitutes an important statement about the tone of this moment, and of the play as a whole:

87

There is one thing which annoys me, it is Estragon's trousers. I naturally asked Suzanne if they fell completely. She told me that they were held up halfway. They should not, absolutely not, that's how it is at that point, he is not even conscious of the great wound inflicted on this touching final tableau, there are absolutely no grounds for objections, they would be of the same order as the preceding ones. The spirit of the piece, to the degree that it has any, is that nothing is more grotesque than the tragic, and it must be expressed until the end, and especially at the end. I have a stack of other reasons for wanting this effect not to be ruined but I will spare you them. Be only kind enough to restore it as indicated in the text and as always allowed for in the course of rehearsals, and let the trousers fall completely around his ankles. That must seem stupid to you but for me it is capital. (Gontarski 1992, p. xiv)

It might be said that the revised text's cutting of Vladimir's business with his (that is, Lucky's) hat backs away from laughter. Yet insofar as this ensures that, as the editors note, 'the stillness is not broken' (1993, p. 171), and the spectator's attention is therefore not divided, the moment could be said to be rendered potentially *funnier*, and the switch from redemption to fallen trousers more naked. It would, in more than one sense, be even more deadpan. The comic pattern of dialogue, complete with a mishearing gag, is certainly unrelenting:

VLADIMIR: We'll hang ourselves tomorrow. (*Pause.*) Unless Godot comes.
ESTRAGON: And if he comes?
VLADIMIR: We'll be saved.
ESTRAGON: Well? Shall we go?
VLADIMIR: Pull on your trousers.
ESTRAGON: What?
VLADIMIR: Pull on your trousers.
ESTRAGON: You want me to pull off my trousers?
VLADIMIR: Pull ON your trousers.
ESTRAGON: (*Realizing his trousers are down*) Ah yes!

(*He pulls up his trousers.*)
VLADIMIR: (*Looking up*) Well? Shall we go?
ESTRAGON: (*Looking down*) Yes, let's go.
(*They do not move. Silence.*)
CURTAIN

(1993, p. 85)

Paradoxically, perhaps, it is Estragon's very unconsciousness of his indignity which ensures our emotional engagement – his clownishness, in fact. For that quality makes itself felt here as a kind of stoicism. 'I can't go on like this', says Estragon. 'That's what you think', replies Vladimir (p. 94). And if this final tableau is touching (as Beckett wanted it to be), it is not despite the 'great wound' inflicted by the falling trousers, but because of it. This is one good reason why *Waiting for Godot* is a tragicomedy.

CHAPTER 4

IN COMPANY – POZZO AND LUCKY

POZZO AND PSYCHOLOGY

Ruby Cohn's memory of the first production of *En attendant Godot* testifies to the stylistic and moral jolt caused by the arrival of Pozzo and Lucky:

> What was new was the eruption of a master / slave pair into cabaret patter. The first Pozzo / Lucky entrance smacked of circus – the driving hand delayed by the long rope connecting the two men. An overburdened Lucky could be milked for farce, but not if he had to fall offstage when Pozzo jerked the rope. And once Pozzo / Blin asserted his cruel presence, the effect was too disturbing for cabaret. Why were these two couples in the same play? Later Blin explained that he intended surprise in the Pozzo / Lucky entrances, but what he achieved was dislocation. (1986, p. 17)

The dislocation continues throughout the play. It is, as Cohn implies, first of all generic. If, as Beckett himself wrote to Roger Blin, there is nothing more grotesque than the tragic, then it is the pseudocouple Pozzo and Lucky who bear the tragic strain through *Godot*. As befits the play's 'tragic relief' (States 1978, p. 62), grotesque Pozzo is at once the cruellest and the funniest of the characters, both the most absurd and, with Lucky, the one who offers himself most obviously to allegorical or representative interpretation. The play gives us our cue, and critics have followed. 'He's all humanity' (p. 83); he's Cain and Lucky Abel (or possibly the other way round); Lucky is Mind at the End of its Tether; Pozzo is a Nazi overlord and Lucky a conquered subject; Pozzo is an Irish Victorian landlord and Lucky his downtrodden peasant; they are Master and Slave in the Hegelian dialectic of world history. When Lucky leads in Pozzo, they bring Big Ideas with them. It would be wrong (as we have already seen in earlier chapters) to treat these ideas merely as red herrings, but they are the ones (to stick with fish) that will always get away. This play, as we know by now, is like that.

Pozzo is a paradox. He is, as I have just indicated, the figure who is most open to interpretation by way of exterior reference, philosophical or historical: he can be made to stand for this or that. As a symbiont within a pseudocouple, he is not understandable outside his relation to his fellow. He is, thus, readily perceived within a multiplicity of possible patterns. Yet it is also the case that, of the four men on stage, he is the one who is most interesting as a *character*, and who offers most rewards to a conventional, character-based reading. He is the one who most compellingly *invites* such a reading. That reading, it's true, will not take us so very far: he is not Prince Hamlet, nor Hedda Gabler. But he is the only one of the four who fetches up, entirely out of the blue, in another Beckett text. The narrator of *Texts for Nothing* 5 (written, in French, in March 1951) asks: 'Why did Pozzo leave home, he had a castle and retainers'. Or rather, it seems that a voice from elsewhere asks the narrator (hence, perhaps, the absence of a question mark). The narrator comments: 'Insidious question, to remind me I'm in the dock' (Beckett 1995, p. 118). It is also a good question, though – an interesting and a plausible one for the spectator of *Godot*. Pozzo gives an answer in the play. He is, he says, 'bringing [Lucky] to the fair, where I hope to get a good price for him' (p. 32). But that is not quite the answer that we want, any more than it was the answer Sir Ralph Richardson wanted when he annoyed the playwright by requesting 'the low-down on Pozzo, his home address and curriculum vitae' (qtd in Knowlson 1996, p. 412). The actor, understandably, wants something from which motivation can be inferred, at least the actor working within postwar Anglo-American theatre-culture.

We have already noted Beckett's antipathy to such approaches, and our examination of the play has amply demonstrated why such an antipathy is justified. Yet when Beckett wrote to his trusted American director (and friend) Alan Schneider, in December 1955, with some suggestions to help Schneider's actors, his observations nevertheless point to psychology as a key. Here is Beckett on Pozzo:

> He is a hypomaniac and the only way to play him is to play him mad. The difficulty always experienced by actors with this role (apart from its mechanics which are merely complicated) results I think from their efforts to clarify it and to give it a unity and a continuity which it simply cannot receive. In other words they try to establish it from without. The result at the best is lifelessness and dulness. Pozzo's sudden changes of tone, mood, behaviour, etc., may I suppose be related to what is going on about him, but their source is in the dark of his own inner upheavals and confusions. The temptation is to minimize an irresponsibility and discontinuity which should on the contrary be stressed. [. . .] Such an understanding of the part is perhaps a lot to ask of an actor, but I am convinced it is the only proper one and, what is more, the only possibly effective one. Played in any other way Pozzo is just dead, artificial and tedious. (Harmon 1998, p. 6)

To establish the character from *within* is a particular challenge when the playwright gives so little information – and that fragmentary – for the actor to work with psychologically; also as the playwright, when himself the director, is concerned almost exclusively with externals. As Jonathan Kalb writes: 'Because Beckett is so reluctant to discuss the psychological motivations of his characters, generally communicating his wishes through line-readings and [. . .] highly specific blocking [. . .], his actors *must* work from external considerations inward' (1989, pp. 42–3).

This cannot be said to be merely an actor's problem. Actors, as I have already noted, are readers too. It is obvious that searching for a non-existent life-history for the character will not help. There is no reason to disbelieve what Beckett said in an early public statement about the play: 'I know no more about the characters than what they say, what they do, and what happens to them. [. . .] I was able to get to know them a little only at a great distance from the need to understand' (Moorjani 1998, p. 54). However when Beckett came to direct the play in 1975, he made significant moves, apparent in the revised text of the play, if not to indicate the origin of Pozzo's 'inner upheavals and confusions', at least to clarify the nature of the 'discontinuities' that they cause.

THE NEW POZZO

In 1953 Roger Blin, as Pozzo, costumed himself 'like an English gentleman farmer' (McMillan and Fehsenfeld 1988, p. 71). While the other characters were 'dowdy and broken-down in the extreme, Blin's costume [. . .] was clean and new' (Bradby 2001, p. 56). In London, Peter Hall's Pozzo, Peter Bull, was more clownish, with loud check suit and overcoat, wing-collar and plus-fours, but similarly prosperous, if not aristocratic. The pattern was set. Not surprisingly, most productions still follow the sharp differentiation of social rank through costume. Beckett's own, however, did not. Carl Raddatz, his 1975 Berlin Pozzo, was costumed with a shabbiness comparable to that of the others on the stage. The principle of complementarity in the costuming of the pseudocouple operated here, as with Vladimir and Estragon, and this further meshed Pozzo with his fellows. This already introduces an extra comic note, for as Ruby Cohn observes, 'his boasts and grand manner are ludicrous when belied by his shabby clothes' (1980, p. 261). In the San Quentin Drama Workshop production of 1984, which Beckett supervised, Pozzo was even more run-down: 'he wears no socks, he has holed knees in his trousers, he is much closer to Didi and Gogo [than] [. . .] before' (Duckworth 1987, pp. 185–6).

This is a new Pozzo, and Colin Duckworth, so hostile to what he sees as 'the New *Godot*' of the revised text, registers it with irritation. Interviewing Rick Cluchey, Pozzo in the San Quentin production, Duckworth notes that Pozzo has 'lost some of his viciousness and sadism [. . .]: there's been a kind of "nicification" of Pozzo's character in this production' (1987, p. 185). Cluchey recalls, 'I remember Beckett saying of Pozzo, "I don't want any more of this overbearing landowner, all this barking"' (qtd in Duckworth 1987, p. 182). Asmus reports that in Berlin:

> Beckett makes it clear that Pozzo is not to be played as a superior figure (as he usually is). Instead, all four characters should be equal. Pozzo is, so to speak, a proletarian Pozzo. He plays the lord – magnanimous, frightening – but only because he is unsure of himself. (McMillan and Fehsenfeld 1988, p. 141)

Asmus himself developed the psychological approach in interview with Jonathan Kalb:

> Is it a psychological explanation [. . .] if you tell the actor he overcompensates? Pozzo is a character who has to overcompensate. That's why he overdoes things, has a tendency to describe the sky and so on as very big, why he tries to impress people, and this overcompensation has to do with a deep insecurity within him. Those were things Beckett said, psychological terms that he used (Kalb 1989, p. 175)

However, when Asmus recounts to Lois Oppenheim how, in his own production in Copenhagen, he conceived of a Pozzo who 'was not the bombastic, loud landowner, but a very, very normal person – just a lonely man who wanted to join some other people at a party or in a conversation, and he didn't speak the same code' (Oppenheim 1994, p. 41), Duckworth's charge of 'nicification' seems justified. With this sentimentalized conception, we have come a long way from Pozzo as Nazi slave-driver. Or indeed from Beckett's overcompensatory 'hypomaniac'.

The 'new Pozzo', then, is a markedly more vulnerable figure. The problem with 'psychologizing' him, however, is not that it unfortunately (though inevitably) produces a sympathetic sort of fellow but that it abstracts the character from the comic texture in which he figures dramatically. Perhaps surprisingly, this comic texture is far from unreceptive of Big Ideas. On the contrary, what we have already identified, in Chapter 2, as the dominant idea governing Pozzo and Lucky, has comedy implicit within it. Once we have recognized this, we do not need a description of Pozzo's psychological condition any more complex than the one Beckett provided for his actors in Berlin.

MAKING AN IMPRESSION

In Chapter 2 I noted the central relevance to the Pozzo–Lucky pseudocoupling of the master–slave dialectic of Hegel. In the words of Alexandre Kojève, mediator of these ideas to mid-century France, the master can ratify his own identity as master 'only by recognition from one whom he recognizes as worthy of recognizing him. [. . .] But the Slave is for him an animal or a thing'. 'Hence, he is recognized by someone whom he does not recognize'. 'The Master's attitude, therefore, is an existential impasse' (1969, p. 19). Kojève calls this impasse tragic; Beckett figures it, in the person of Pozzo, as comic. Either way, the situation is intrinsically theatrical. The 'Hegelian demand for recognition' is, as Angela Moorjani puts it, 'no more or less than the dependence of actors in any play on the eyes and ears of an audience in order to exist' (2003, p. 74). This is why, as Beckett told Michael Rudman, 'Pozzo is a bluff [. . .] always trying to make an impression' (qtd in Croall 2005, p. 115). The way to make an impression, in the theatre, is through performance.

Pozzo's ontological problem (that is, his problem about being) is rendered comic because it makes itself felt in the first place as a *social* problem. We recognize the dilemma. He is the master, the landowner (he must be because he says he is) with a manor; he is proud of all his possessions. (In the revised text he sacrifices his pipe, but gains an offstage Steinway; you do not have to be a pianist to feel that even a dedicated smoker would accept this *quid pro quo*.) One of these possessions is his carrier. To treat the carrier as an animal is gratifying in that it gives a sense of absolute power, but in the long run frustrating because, insofar as Lucky plays as cast, he cannot reflect his master's glory back upon him. When Pozzo comes upon Vladimir and Estragon, it is a great opportunity. These two are clearly (by the look of their clothes) his social inferiors and they are on his land (or at least he can tell them they are, even if they're not). On the other hand, they are not potential slaves, so their recognition is well worth having, especially as there are no alternatives and his sense of self, we infer, is dribbling away as fast as theirs. He must engage them sympathetically but firmly. This takes exploitation to another, more refined level – if he can bring the performance off.

It is a performance that involves the simultaneous appeasement of conflicting psychic needs: to be recognized and acknowledged as Master, and yet to maintain a relation which does not drive away the inferior partner(s). This is the balancing-act of one who can exist only as a symbiont yet whose self-projection must display masterful independence. Overcompensation is the chief symptom, and no one can say he doesn't make an impression. It is no wonder that the playwright thought disunity and discontinuity should be the actor's watchwords.

After he warns the 'guests' to be wary of the slave (who is 'wicked' but being kept under control for their good too), the performance begins. It entails first of all being frightening, just to make sure these two know who is in charge: '(*terrifying voice*). I am Pozzo! (*Silence.*) Pozzo! (*Silence.*) Does that name mean nothing to you? (*Silence.*) I say does that name mean nothing to you?' (p. 22). The revised text adds, after the announcement of the name, that he '*drops the rope and advances, driving them back and apart*' (1993, p. 21). The ensuing routine from Vladimir and Estragon, as they remove their hats, '*pretending to search*', nicely punctures the idiotic self-importance. Vladimir's conciliatory punchline, 'I once knew a family called Gozzo. The mother had the clap' (p. 23), is a fine unintentional slap at dignity. But Pozzo is unphased, and rapidly identifies these two as beings whose recognition of himself would fulfil his immediate requirements very well – not of course that they are exactly his equals: 'You are human beings none the less. (*He puts on his glasses.*) As far as one can see. (*He takes off his glasses.*) Of the same species as myself. (*He bursts into an enormous laugh.*) Of the same species as Pozzo! Made in God's image!' (p. 23). It would be wrong though, to put them at their ease just yet. So he asks, '*peremptor[il]y*', 'Who is Godot?' and presses his questions. They are, after all, on his land. But it is the moment for magnanimity, and then for pointing out how magnanimous one's gestures are, under the circumstances:

> POZZO: The road is free to all.
> VLADIMIR: That's how we looked at it.
> POZZO: It's a disgrace. But there you are.
> ESTRAGON: Nothing we can do about it.
> POZZO: (*with magnanimous gesture*). Let's say no more about it. (*He jerks the rope.*) Up pig!
>
> (p. 23)

The mutual gestures of the puffed-up master and the wily fore-lock-tugging underlings are no doubt as old as comedy itself. But now the *need* that the parties have for each other – as audience, as companions – is much plainer, and cannot merely be thought of as social convenience. When Beckett said of *Godot* that 'it's all symbiosis', he meant what he said: not just two symbiotic pairs but two pairs which are themselves symbiotic with each other, forming a larger and more complex symbiote. 'Gentlemen, I am happy to have met you. [. . .] Yes, yes, sincerely happy' (p. 24). We believe him.

Served by Lucky, Pozzo proceeds to picnic, making pleasant conversation the while. His watch informs him that he has been travelling for six hours 'and never a soul in sight'. The 'pig' Lucky doesn't count as a soul, but these two 'gentlemen' do. Even so, the trick is to understate his need for their company and to keep them in their place while engaging them politely and more or less warmly: 'Yes, gentlemen, I cannot go for long without the society of my likes (*he puts on his glasses and looks at the two likes*) even when the likeness is an imperfect one. [. . .] That is why, with your permission, I propose to dally with you a moment, before I venture any further' (p. 24). The pompous locutions are meant to cow them further.

Vladimir and Estragon cautiously approach Lucky, examining and describing him in a cross-talk routine. But on Pozzo's command they (in the revised text) '*scurry back to the stone*' (1993, p. 25). By now, they know their place, and Pozzo has been

97

satisfied of that. When Estragon tries to cadge Pozzo's chicken bones the mutually agreed statuses are clear:

> ESTRAGON: (*timidly*). Please, sir . . .
> POZZO: What is it, my good man?
> ESTRAGON: Er . . . you've finished with the . . . er . . . you
> don't need the . . . er . . . bones, sir?

(p. 26)

Always tickled by the semiotics of status, Pozzo is enraptured with irony when Estragon, after the bones, addresses Lucky as 'Mister'. Throughout much of the interaction of Pozzo with Vladimir and Estragon, the silent Lucky is the focal point. For the waiting pair he is the fixed object of puzzlement and speculation, of outrage, pity and wonder. As far as the master is concerned, Lucky serves as an ever-present unprotesting stooge for the performance which constitutes Pozzo's self-presentation.

When Lucky 'refuses' the bones, Pozzo comments ('*to himself* in the revised text), 'Nice business it'd be if he fell sick on me!' (1993, p. 26) and Vladimir explodes in outrage at the treatment of the carrier: '(*stutteringly resolute*). To treat a man . . . [. . .] like that . . . I think that . . . no . . . a human being . . . no . . . it's a scandal!' The outburst simultaneously anticipates our own responses and forestalls them, as we recognize the comic intention at work in Estragon's reaction. Even as he gnaws the bones, he agrees with Vladimir '*not to be outdone*' (p. 27). Pozzo seems genuinely puzzled, patronizing Vladimir by asking how old he is. He starts a pantomime on the phrase 'I must be getting on'. He rises, then decides to stay. But this is a problem of self-presentation, which involves an attempted dialogue with his uninterested audience: 'But how am I to sit down now, without affectation, now that I have risen? Without appearing to – how shall I say – without appearing to falter. (*To Vladimir.*) I beg your pardon? (*Silence.*) Perhaps you didn't speak? (*Silence.*) It's of no importance' (p. 28). Pozzo's anxiety about his audience issues in a continuous commentary designed to engage their attention: 'I hope I'm not driving you away. Wait a little longer, you'll never regret it' (p. 28). When Vladimir wants to go, he keeps him there by asking about Godot. Desperate for their company, he is always on his guard against revealing that, and for this reason his every comment has a patronizing rider:

> VLADIMIR: You're being asked a question.
> POZZO: (*delighted*). A question! Who? What? A moment ago you were calling me sir, in fear and trembling. Now you're asking me questions. No good will come of this!
>
> (p. 29)

The comedy of social status now merges with the comedy of metatheatre, as Pozzo moves towards the first of his four inset performances. The question, from Estragon, is about why Lucky doesn't put down his bags. Pozzo seizes on it as the occasion for an informal performance. He will deliver his answer, but the audience's full attention has first of all to be secured: 'Is everybody ready? Is everybody looking at me? (*He looks at Lucky, jerks the rope. Lucky raises his head.*) Will you look at me, pig!' (p. 30). About to undertake a vocal performance, he makes use of his vaporizer for his throat and, assuring them that he doesn't like 'talking in a vacuum', announces his readiness. By which time, of course, he has forgotten the question. The answer, when it comes, is delivered in no less than five versions, which are merely rhetorical variants of the first: 'He wants to impress me, so that I'll keep him' (p. 31). The whole sequence is a comedy of bathos: expectation is absurdly pumped up, then punctured.

Nevertheless, the fact that Lucky weeps ('Old dogs have more dignity') when Pozzo announces his intention of 'bringing him to the fair, where I hope to get a good price for him' (p. 32) suggests that Pozzo's answer to the question, in one or all of its variants, is true. When Lucky kicks Estragon, who has been invited by Pozzo to comfort him, Pozzo takes this as an opportunity to expatiate on the 'tears of the world' – another little performance which swells grandly but ends up in glum self-cancellation: 'Let us not then speak ill [. . .] Let us not speak well [. . .] Let us not speak of it at all' (p. 33). The account of his relations with Lucky (which we considered in Chapter 2) reawakens Vladimir's earlier outrage, with Estragon jumping on the moral bandwagon. Vladimir's outburst

('After having sucked all the good out of him you chuck him away like a . . . like a banana skin' (p. 34)) provokes Pozzo's third performance. He grows increasingly agitated, then: '(*groaning, clutching his head*). I can't bear it . . . any longer . . . the way he goes on . . . you've no idea . . . it's terrible . . . he must go . . . (*he waves his arms*) . . . I'm going mad . . . (*he collapses, his head in his hands*)' (p. 34). Without our conception of Pozzo as performer, and with only the standard text to hand, we might suppose that this bizarre reaction has something to do with the mysterious symbiosis of the pseudocouple. But at just this point the revised text adds a direction to confirm what is going on: '*gives furtive looks from behind his hand to measure effect*' (1993, p. 32).

This striking performance has the requisite effect. Vladimir executes a comic *volte-face*: now the pathetic slave is to blame ('How dare you! It's abominable! Such a good master! Crucify him like that! After so many years! Really!'). Having stooged his carrier successfully, and fooled the susceptible clown, Pozzo stages an immediate recovery ('Gentlemen, I don't know what came over me. [. . .] I don't remember exactly what it was, but you may be sure there wasn't a word of truth in it'). But he is left with the dilemma of maintaining his image of mastery ('Do I look like a man that can be made to suffer? Frankly?' (p. 34)). Fortunately for him, the dilemma dissolves when he finds he has lost his pipe.

Pozzo's last performance, which is something of a set-piece, is yet to come. Before it he declares that '[a] great calm descends' and waxes mythological: 'Pan sleeps'. He generously sympathizes with the situation of those waiting for Godot, and, with Estragon's help, stages a charming scene which enables him to sit down again: 'Be seated, sir, I beg of you.' 'No, no, I wouldn't think of it! (*Pause. Aside.*) Ask me again' (p. 36). Without theatre, it seems, Pozzo cannot negotiate even the most basic activity. This being so, his problem is how to maintain dignity and respect. He must be magnanimous. So, after rallying his audience, he resolves to explain the twilight to them. 'He doesn't want to lose their company' (McMillan and Fehsenfeld 1988, p. 141), insisted Beckett as director; all the same, Pozzo will not tolerate a merely passive audience. They must all look at the sky, even the dozing 'pig', Lucky. His speech goes through the rhetorical paint-box: he asks a question, answers it, harks back, alternates lyrical and prosaic tones, gestures mimetically, enacting a rich, slow progression and moving suddenly to a vibrant onomatopoeic climax. It is clear that the tonal variety and discontinuity upon which Beckett early insisted for the role are essential characteristics of Pozzo as performer. What he ends by describing is an apocalyptic version of what Vladimir and Estragon experience every night. And it all ends in gloom – not just the night, but the rhetorician's faith in his own self-sustaining powers. Indeed the progress of the light through the day tracks the speaker's mood as he performs:

> But – (*hand raised in admonition*) – but behind this veil of gentleness and peace night is charging (*vibrantly*) and will burst upon us (*snaps his fingers*) pop! like that! (*his inspiration leaves him*) just when we least expect it. (*Silence. Gloomily.*) That's how it is on this bitch of an earth.
> *Long silence.*
>
> (p. 38)

By this time his stage audience has caught on to what Pozzo needs, and so to his particular brand of vulnerability. They are at first gracefully consolatory, then ready to be cued into a scenario of critical comment. We understand from Vladimir's response that this is a delayed-reaction joke:

> POZZO: How did you find me? (*Vladimir and Estragon look at him blankly.*) Good? Fair? Middling? Poor? Positively bad?
> VLADIMIR: (*first to understand*). Oh very good, very very good.

'*Thumb up*' (1993, p. 36), adds the revised text. Pozzo goes fishing, and is amusingly rewarded:

> POZZO: (*fervently*). Bless you, gentlemen, bless you! (*Pause.*) I have such need of encouragement! (*Pause.*) I weakened a little towards the end, you didn't notice?

VLADIMIR: Oh perhaps just a teeny weeny little bit.
ESTRAGON: I thought it was intentional.

(p. 38)

It is a generous response. Pozzo has made his impression, to be sure, but only at the cost of revealing his vulnerability.

To say that Pozzo 'performs' gives the wrong impression because it suggests that he feels he has the choice in assuming a particular mode of behaviour. But in his case there is no stable self which performs. Rather, as we have just seen, the self is constantly and repeatedly constructed *through* performance. If he fails to make an impression, nothing of him will remain, and nothing of him will properly exist. The humour of this middle sequence of Act I results from Pozzo's obligation to combine the imperative of performance – which implies an absolute dependence on whomsoever can be imposed upon to compose the audience – with the maintenance of an elevated social status. As ever in *Godot*, the comedy, as it is concerned with *being*, is being serious.

THE KNOOK

When Pozzo describes Lucky's intriguing history he recalls his own need, in the face of 'Professional worries', for 'Beauty, grace, truth of the first water, I knew they were all beyond me. So I took a knook' (p. 33). The moment is amusing because, although Vladimir is as puzzled as we are, Pozzo assumes that anyone listening would know what a 'knook' is. In fact (the reference books assure us) Beckett invented the word. (Presumably the 'k' is sounded, for reasons of euphony.) In *En attendant Godot*, after Pozzo's revelation of his bald head and Lucky's teeming hair, Vladimir asks what a 'knouk' (as it is in French) is. (This question and Pozzo's answer were not translated in *Waiting for Godot*.) Pozzo wonders patronizingly if Vladimir is not from these parts, or is merely out of touch: 'People used to have buffoons. Now they have knooks. Those who can afford them, that is' (editors' translation in 1993, p. 122).

The knook is a teacher: 'Guess who taught me all these beautiful things', asks Pozzo (p. 33). He is associated with (as one of

James Joyce's heroes puts it) all those big words which make us so unhappy. But those things are thought of as existing only in the past – along with Lucky's usefulness. Beauty, grace and truth are in ruins, and so is their conduit, Lucky. The knook is now a carrier, and in 'reality he carries like a pig' because it's 'not his job' (p. 31). He retains, however, his function as an entertainer, a buffoon, and a living sign of his master's social status. (It is ironic that in this play of clowns the ex-professional is the least amusing figure.) Are we to think here of the Shakespearean fool, the witty truth-teller living under threat of punishment or abandonment but who will nonetheless not be silenced? 'Take heed, sirrah – the whip' (*King Lear* I.iv.109). There are, after all, many partners in literature less convincing as pseudocouples than Lear and his Fool.

If Lucky tells the truth about the world of *Waiting for Godot*, it is through his dance and his Think that he does so. This is not to underrate his dramatic presence from the moment of his driven entrance. That is not something we are ever allowed to ignore, given Pozzo's persistent commands and the curiosity of Vladimir and Estragon. Lucky is, as we have seen, the point of dramatic reference which enables the comic presentation of Pozzo's brutality and Estragon's greed and self-seeking servility; also of his and Vladimir's sentimental compassion and gullibility. As a stage presence in himself, he is, in the words of the *Grove Companion*, 'the image of suffering inhumanity' (Ackerley and Gontarski 2004, p. 329). In Act II the paradoxical power of the slave over the ruined master is an unforgettable idea. Nevertheless it is in Act I, when he becomes the focus of attention as a performer, that Lucky moves to the centre of the play.

Pozzo acknowledges that the men have been 'civil' to him, and – 'liberal' as he is, by his own generous admission – he is 'tortured' by the idea that he has not done enough 'to cheer them up' (p. 39). The talk of liberality and torture ('I shall suffer, no doubt about that') is accompanied by a jerk on Lucky's rope and a brandishing of the whip. Entertainment is offered. Estragon wishes Lucky to 'dance first and think afterwards'. 'It's the natural order', Pozzo confirms (pp. 39–40). Lucky dances, encores; Estragon is not impressed; Pozzo describes the decline:

'He used to dance the farandole, the fling, the brawl, the jig, the fandango, and even the hornpipe. He capered. For joy. Now that's the best he can do. Do you know what he calls it?' (p. 40).

In his Berlin production, and therefore in the revised text, Beckett highlighted the name of the dance very distinctly by cutting the comic guesses at it, and then a whole page of the dialogue which follows Pozzo's answer to his own question (pp. 40–1), so that the revised text reads thus:

> POZZO: The Net. He thinks he's entangled in a net.
> *Long silence.*
> VLADIMIR: (*Stands.*) Nothing happens, nobody comes, nobody goes, it's awful!
>
> (1993, p. 38)

The long silence is in fact one of 12 tableaux, which Beckett referred to as *Wartestellen* (waiting points or 'moments of stillness'), introduced into this production. (A full list can be found in McMillan and Fehsenfeld 1988, pp. 115–16.) These tableaux serve not only to punctuate the action but also to create a particular resonance, as here with the image of the net. The effect is to generalize the image: it now applies to all of them, not just to Lucky. The metaphor of imprisonment was in the mind of Beckett the director. In his production notebook, he referred to the '2 caged dynamics' of Estragon ('sluggish') and Vladimir ('restless'), and in another notebook he first contemplated, then cancelled, the image of 'Faint shadow of bars on stage floor' (see McMillan and Fehsenfeld 1988, p. 115). A net yields to movement, as Lucky's dance should demonstrate, where bars do not. It permits the trapped creature to dissipate its energy and exhaust itself. It leads inevitably to the incarceration of the creature behind those bars, if not to the kill.

THE THINK

One of the best jokes in the performance history of *Godot* is Roger Blin's description of Lucky to Jean Martin (who was to play him in the first *En attendant Godot*) as a part with 'only one line' (qtd in Aslan 1988, p. 32). As the Think, Lucky's only 'line', has no full stop, it cannot even be thought of as a sentence. Nonetheless, it is as an abortive sentence, which describes itself as 'unfinished', that it has been most usefully considered. The standard analysis of the structure of the Think is by Anselm Atkins, who divides it into three distinct parts: (1) 'the unfinished protasis [the clause stating the condition in a conditional sentence] of a theological or philosophical argument'; (2) 'the last half of an *objection* [. . .] to the unfinished demonstration in the first' (which itself has three subdivisions); (3) 'begins as a second objection in parallel' to (2), with two phases, but soon 'discards all syntax and lapses into complete aphasia [inability to communicate]' (1987, pp. 95–6). Lawrence Graver, who writes eloquently about the Think, summarizes its message in a sentence: 'if God exists, He is absent, unresponsive to us, and despite heralded strides in nutrition, personal hygiene, medicine, and communication, human beings waste and pine, shrink and dwindle' (2004, p. 47). The most authoritative analytic framework of all identifies three sections: (1) 'Indifferent heaven' – from the opening to 'but not so fast' (pp. 42–3); (2) 'Dwindling man' – from 'considering what is more' to 'and the facts are there' (pp. 43–4); (3) 'Earth abode of stones' – from 'and considering' to 'I resume' (p. 44). These are followed by a 'cadenza' (pp. 44–5) which reiterates themes before fragmenting in repetition (1993, p. 132).

The main theme of the speech, which, as Beckett himself pointed out, is not as difficult as it may seem, is the vanity of striving for knowledge – which appears in the form of pairs of cod academic authorities – and the ultimate futility of physical culture, in the face of the inevitable decline of human beings. The discourse of traditional, if naïve, Christian belief is present in the shape of a personal God and elemental apocalyptic imagery. The earth as an 'abode of stones' (p. 44), barren, featureless and indifferent, seems essential to the vision. That vision is not satiric; indeed it is characterized by a frantic pathos attaching to the 'labours unfinished' (p. 43) and the 'labours lost' (p. 44) of the various researchers, absurd though these labours are. Such labours may remind us of the 'difficult birth' of Vladimir's final speech, as indeed their 'unfinished' nature might too; just as the

calm may remind us of the aching desirability of 'cawm' throughout the play; the fire of the apocalyptic flames of Pozzo's twilight;
the tears of those shed by Lucky; the stones of Estragon's permanent aspirations to immobility on (and with) *his* stone; the
light to that which gleams an instant in Pozzo's last speech; and
'the skull in Connemara' (p. 44) to the last end towards which all
the shrinking and wasting lead all of us. When Beckett directed
the play in Berlin he began rehearsals, to the surprise of the
company, with this monologue, 'for it was here, he said, that the
"threads and themes" of the play "are being gathered together"'
(Graver 2004, p. 46). In the light (as the speech itself puts it) of
this gathering together, one might turn the case around and view
the Think as the *womb* of the play, the virtual container of the
text that contains it. The whole play, then, is a difficult birth out
of this speech. Or perhaps one might think of the Think as an
eruption of the play's unconscious, accessed by and through the
knook in the frenzy of his waking nightmare. It is no wonder the
others set upon him to stop him.

These speculations might be found suggestive. The analyses
cited are certainly sound and helpful. Yet there is a particular
irony, of which I am the victim too, about academic critics,
whom the Think mournfully parodies, addressing themselves to
the task of ascertaining order in an apparently chaotic speech –
just as Puncher and Wattmann, and Testew and Cunard, not to
mention Fartov and Belcher, and Steinweg and Peterman,
devote their 'labours unfinished' and 'labours lost' to understanding the plight of humans in a godforsaken universe. This
irony is not merely incidental. The problem of the relation of
chaos and form, clarity and unintelligibility, impinges at every
level in any consideration of the Think. This chaotic tirade is
obsessed by the promised perception of order. In her discussion
of the speech as a problem of performance, Jane R. Goodall
restates the case:

> The remnants of Lucky's memory are organized around a dis-
> course whose logic tells of the inescapable consequential link
> between measurability and diminution, yet the speech in
> which he attempts to recapture this calls for attention as the

most visibly energetic and climactic episode in all of Beckett's dramatic works. (2006, p. 188)

It is a paradox familiar in Beckett's writing. Nothing is as energizing as the prospect of ending; nothing as agitating as the promise of 'cawm'; nothing more vivifying than the onset of mortification. And nothing more chaotically energetic than the drive towards order.

Thus critics who (genuinely) clarify structure and argument hastily qualify their analyses, insisting, as they must, on Lucky's delirium, his desperation, his vehemence amidst the coruscating torrent of his words. Such qualifications are not open to performers, however. Directors and actors are obliged to make fundamental decisions about intelligibility and potential impact. For example, the more intelligible the Think, the more available for laughter it is likely to be. Its parody of academic discourses becomes more clearly audible – not just in the citation of the pairs of cod-scholarly authorities but in the syntactical framework, a parody of academic argumentation, which is designed to contain this uncontainable tirade. (One need look no further than Lucky's abortive opening – 'On the other hand with regard to –' (p. 42) – which is yet another little comic double to add to all the others in the play.) As Goodall (2006, pp. 190–1) and William Hutchings (2005, pp. 33–4) note, 'mad' professors talking 'technical' gobbledegook were just as much a staple of music hall and vaudeville as the double act. But here the very irrepressibility of Lucky ensures that this comedy passes through the looking-glass into nightmare.

Let us then move to consider contrasting performance options. In fact there is an overlap between analysis and performance. What I referred to above as the most authoritative analytic framework actually derives from the playwright's theatre notebook, compiled in preparation for his Berlin production of 1975. In directing Klaus Herm as Lucky, Beckett emphasized the quality of Lucky's awareness, and clarified his motive. He could watch Pozzo from time to time, as (according to Asmus) 'Beckett explains that Lucky would like to amuse Pozzo. Pozzo would like to get rid of him, but if he finds Lucky touching, he might keep him'. 'And the two others, too. He is not talking simply to himself. He is not completely on his own' (McMillan and Fehsenfeld 1988, p. 139). These directions imply a significant measure of self-awareness and self-control on the part of Lucky. Ruby Cohn reports the results of the clarification: 'Usually rushed through as nonsense, this mono- logue became a miracle of intelligibility. [. . .] Lucky-Herm began slowly [. . .]; he quickened the tempo for the first counter- argument [dwindling man] [. . .]; always articulate, he sped to the second counter-argument [earth abode of stones] [. . .]. He finally raves in a frenzied coda' (1980, p. 264). When Jonathan Kalb asked Herm why he spoke the Think 'much slower and more sensibly than most other actors', Herm explained in terms of character-motivation: 'Because Lucky wants to express himself clearly. That's his desperate attempt, now that he is obliged to talk: to clear something up. [. . .] So he's always trying to reorganize, concentrate on the next point' (Kalb 1989, pp. 200–1). As David Bradby remarks: 'The audience should feel the despair of a man whose pride once lay in the "pretty" way he could voice his thoughts, but who now finds the control of his words slipping away' (2001, p. 114). The clown-facet was suggested too, as in the other elements of this production. In his review, Martin Esslin noted that 'Klaus Herm's Lucky has the white face of a clown like Grock' (1976, p. 99).

This conception and delivery of the speech are at almost the opposite end of the spectrum to what is probably the most famous performance (captured in a sound recording, just as Herm's was to be). Where Herm focused on motivation, Jean Martin, the first French Lucky, conceived the role physically, working inward from the symptoms of one suffering from advanced Parkinson's disease – trembling and slavering. Directed by Roger Blin, friend of the visionary poet, director and theorist Antonin Artaud, Martin produced an astonishing, Artaudian, rendering of the Think. Odette Aslan describes it:

> Jean Martin began by delivering his text slowly, syllable by syl-
> lable, in a monotonous tone that gradually became choppy.
> Then his pace picked up like a machine run amuck; his voice

emitted sharp uncontrolled notes, repeated syllables making the discourse skid, an acceleration leading to incomprehensibility. (1988, p. 35)

The mechanical metaphor is unavoidable. Self-control was never an issue here, as it was with Herm. David Bradby describes Martin's beginning as 'evoking a damp motor engine stuttering unreliably into life', and he further observes: 'the words emerged at the same rhythm as the trembling spasms which convulsed his body, so that the whole speech was imprinted with the image of physical breakdown' (2001, p. 62). Clearly psychology was not the point. The impact of the performance was physically disturbing. Where Herm, under Beckett's direction, played the pseudocoupled carrier, with clear, and simple, psychological motivation, Martin played the brutalized, dehumanized, victim of an unquestioned authority. We could conclude that where Herm played Lucky as character, Martin played Lucky as iconic presence. With Herm we are to sympathize with the plight of a particular man, losing control of what he had once mastered; with Martin we register with physicalized intensity the symbolic outcome of an impersonal brutality.

In the case of Lucky, then, performance options again raise the question of the *nature* of character in *Waiting for Godot*. This is the question we considered at length in our discussion of Vladimir and Estragon. In this instance it is even more tempting to state the terms as an opposition: psychological or stylized? Internal or external? Motive or choreography? There can be no final answer to these questions. But the differing approaches to Lucky's Think suggest that the issue of intelligibility, which I introduced earlier, might take its place alongside these. In doing so it provokes an even larger question – one which invites contemplation of nothing less than the purpose and limitations of art itself. How does the playwright (or indeed the playwright as director) go about evoking the experience of unintelligibility within a medium which – like any other artistic medium – exists in order to suggest the presence of meaning, if not always to make it manifest? How, in the very realm of form, can one effectively and truly insinuate form*lessness*?

There is of course no solution. Nevertheless *Godot* does offer a response to the impasse. In a review of 1938, Beckett asserted that 'art has nothing to do with clarity, does not dabble in the clear and does not make clear' (1983, p. 94). By the time of *Godot* he may not have shifted from this position. However, as we saw in Chapter 2, the relation of *Waiting for Godot* to meaning (if I can phrase it in this way) is far more ambiguous – indeed far more *artful* – than anything that earlier claim would suggest. It never leaves us merely *without* clarity. Richard Dutton's observations on Lucky's Think accurately sum up its relation to meaning:

> What makes the speech particularly painful, and perhaps explains the determination of the other characters to silence him, is the fact that even incoherence is not the final answer; if it were possible to be *certain* that nothing had any meaning, that there was no purpose in life, it might also be possible to cultivate a peaceful resignation to the fact. But Lucky's jumble contains just enough echoes of a comprehensible world [. . .] and just enough *potential* themes to make such resignation impossible (1986, pp. 75–6)

Our experience, once again, is a kind of suspension. We grasp for intelligibility but can never confirm it. Sense is made and simultaneously unmade; we are invited, then abandoned. The light gleams an instant, then it's night once more. In 1961 Beckett asserted in interview: 'To find a form that accommodates the mess, that is the task of the artist now' (Graver and Federman 1979, p. 219). If Lucky's Think is a model of the play that contains it, it is because it stands as an attempt to arrive at that paradoxical entity: a form in which the accommodation of 'the mess' does not simultaneously entail a denial of it.

CONCLUSION: THROUGH THE CHARACTERS
TO THE KEY THEMES AND ISSUES

My critical progression in this book could be thought of as indirect. Instead of starting from characters and moving towards what would normally be considered larger concerns – themes, problems, 'issues' – I have reversed that process. My reasons for proceeding in this way should have become clear. In this play, characters, or to be precise, character itself, *is* one of the major concerns and one of the problems which we have needed to identify and address. *Waiting for Godot* is not unique in this. Ironically, its very success, and consequent influence, has ensured that the same could be said of many plays written since the 1950s. Nor is it the first twentieth-century play to render character problematic. But so radical is its operation, so profound its effect and so trickily ambiguous its means, that an initial assumption that character can be treated as a stable entity would severely limit any interpretative approach. It has been more helpful, then, to move *towards* the consideration of character than to start from it.

At the beginning of our investigation I suggested that *Godot* could usefully be approached as an exercise in dramatic minimalism, where the critic might ask how the escapologist-playwright had untied his own hands. The answer to that question, we soon saw, and have seen repeatedly, is: by way of metatheatre – theatrical reflexivity. Where there is nothing to be done, and nothing to do it with, the only remaining resource, playing itself, assumes the centre of attention, and the action becomes an essay in reflexivity. But when one is imprisoned in an infinite sequence of reflections, one's *self* is located nowhere. To put it another way, one is always at least one remove from the experience of full presence. The quintessential creature of the theatre, the actor, is composed of masks. In this sense the actor exists at one remove from presence. Thus the playwright's solution to his minimalist problem is one which involves characters who, if they are not absent, are not in the conventional sense present either. They are, as it were, made up of their performances, and as a result they are always potentially dislocated – from their environment, from each other, from themselves (if they can indeed be spoken of as having selves). Their presence, which is shrinking and dwindling all the time, is maintained by that process of interindependence which their author calls 'pseudocoupling'. The destabilized self is compelled to be *relational*, for it is composed by the essentially performative connection it has with others. Those others are vital as co-performers or audience, or both. It should be clear that we are far away now from the conventional idea of a character, who is conceived of as entering into relations with others, but as nonetheless individual and autonomous prior to those relationships. This play is not like that. In *Godot*, relations compose the character, not vice-versa, and those relations are relentlessly performative.

The nature of the characters, in its turn, presents the reader or spectator with a problem, one which the play pinpoints in its subtitle: *Waiting for Godot* is a 'tragicomedy'. As I have summarized it above, the situation of the characters, exposed in the unforgiving arena of self-performance, is readily perceptible as tragic, involving as it does a lack or a loss. The void of self is the vacuum their natures abhor. Here too, however, the play presents us with a situation of interindependence, for tragedy and comedy together form the last, and (as we have seen) in some ways the most problematic pseudocouple. Presence in the play is continually composed within and by patterns which are recognizably comic. That is, the patterns relate to traditional comic modes. Yet beneath them all, as the play goes on, we feel the increasingly strong undertow of lack and loss, and on occasion that undertow rises to the surface as a powerful wave of tragic feeling: 'They give birth astride of a grave'. Thus time and again – 'your accursed time' as Pozzo calls it – we are left not quite knowing how to *take* these characters. We are left in a state of suspension in respect of genre. Tragicomedy in this play is less a separate hybrid genre than a permanent state of tension between two ancient conventions. In this sense, then, if in no other, we share the experience of the characters: we are suspended in an area of ambiguous perception. But where it leaves them baffled and despondent, it moves us to delight and admiration. 'I don't know what to think any more' (p. 90), says Vladimir. Perhaps we, its audience, can best think of *Waiting for Godot* as a comic catastrophe with 'tragic relief'. That would be a beginning.

FURTHER READING

TEXTS

For further information, see the section on 'Three Editions' in the Introduction. The following texts together form the foundation of any advanced study of the play.

Beckett, S. (1965b), *Waiting for Godot: A Tragicomedy in Two Acts* (2nd edn). London: Faber and Faber.

— (2006), *En attendant Godot / Waiting for Godot: Tragicomedy in 2 Acts: A Bilingual Edition*. New York: Grove Press. The bilingual edition by Faber and Faber is the one generally available in the UK, though it is less attractively designed and laid out. The Grove also has a useful introduction by S. E. Gontarski.

McMillan, D. and Knowlson, J. (eds) (1993), *The Theatrical Notebooks of Samuel Beckett: Vol.1: 'Waiting for Godot', with a Revised Text*. London: Faber and Faber.

REFERENCE, BIOGRAPHY AND CRITICISM

Ackerley, C. J. and Gontarski, S. E. (2006), *The Faber Companion to Samuel Beckett: A Reader's Guide to His Works, Life, and Thought*. London: Faber and Faber. Over 700 pages of short(ish) entries, arranged alphabetically in double columns. Essential reference.

Boxall, P. (ed.) (2000), *Samuel Beckett: 'Waiting for Godot' / 'Endgame': A Reader's Guide to Essential Criticism*. Cambridge: Icon. A history of criticism, with extracts. Extracts are well chosen and extensive. They are linked by editorial commentary which both clarifies critical positions and illuminates the relations between them.

Bradby, D. (2001), *Beckett: 'Waiting for Godot' (Plays in Production)*. Cambridge: Cambridge University Press. A well-illustrated study of the stage-history of the play. Especially interesting on French contexts, and conditions of reception generally.

Cohn, R. (ed.) (1987), *Samuel Beckett, 'Waiting for Godot': A Casebook*. London: Macmillan. Mostly short essays and extracts, organized into three categories: 'The Stage', 'The Study' and 'At Large'. An ideal starting-point, indicating many different perspectives on the play.

Connor, S. (ed.) (1992), *'Waiting for Godot' and 'Endgame': Contemporary Critical Essays*. London: Macmillan. Seven of the essays collected here, from different theoretical perspectives, are on, or partly on, *Godot* – including Wolfgang Iser on comedy and Connor himself on presence. The editorial commentary is also helpful.

Croall, J. (2005), *The Coming of Godot: A Short History of a Masterpiece*. London: Oberon Books. Alternates a history of the play with chapters on the progress of Peter Hall's 2005 revival. An absorbing read, for critic or theatre-goer.

Fletcher, B. S., Fletcher, J., Smith, B. and Bachem, W. (1978), *A Student's Guide to the Plays of Samuel Beckett*. London and Boston: Faber and Faber. Out of print, but still useful reference if you can find it. Notes on *Godot* are on pp. 38–70.

Graver, L. (2004), *Samuel Beckett: 'Waiting for Godot'* (2nd edn). Cambridge: Cambridge University Press. The best short introduction: wide-ranging, humane and informative.

Graver, L. and Federman, R. (eds) (1979), *Samuel Beckett: The Critical Heritage*. London: Routledge and Kegan Paul. Early reviews and responses to *Godot* – French and English – are to be found on pp. 88–115. Essential interviews are also collected here.

Haynes, J. and Knowlson, J. (2003), *Images of Beckett*. Cambridge: Cambridge University Press. Illuminating essays by Knowlson on Beckett's character, his interest in art and his practice as a director of his own plays; all accompanied and illustrated by Haynes's superb photographs.

Kalb, J. (1989), *Beckett in Performance*. Cambridge: Cambridge University Press. Chapter 3 is an important discussion of performance style in *Godot* and other 'early' plays. Also includes illuminating interviews with actors.

Knowlson, J. (1996), *Damned to Fame: The Life of Samuel Beckett*. London: Bloomsbury. The authorized biography, and a great achievement. Chapters 13–16 (pp. 319–417) are the ones most directly relevant to *Godot*; but in truth there is not much in this narrative that is not at least potentially relevant.

McMillan, D. and Fehsenfeld, M. (1988), *Beckett in the Theatre: The Author as Practical Playwright and Director: Vol 1: From 'Waiting for Godot' to 'Krapp's Last Tape'*. London: John Calder. An invaluable sourcebook, with separate chapters on the play (pp. 47–86) and Beckett's own production (pp. 87–161), offering copious information and commentary.

Schlueter, J. and Brater, E. (eds) (1991), *Approaches to Teaching Beckett's 'Waiting for Godot'*. New York: Modern Language Association of America. Twenty-one short essays, classified by approach and prefaced by a section on 'materials'. Valuable as much for learners as for those other learners who happen also to be teachers.

States, B. O. (1978), *The Shape of Paradox: An Essay on 'Waiting for Godot'*. Berkeley, Los Angeles and London: University of California Press. An 'examination of the ways in which shape matters in *Godot*'. Witty, penetrating and generous: still the best monograph on the play.

The production of *Waiting for Godot* directed by Michael Lindsay-Hogg and issued on DVD as part of the RTE *Beckett on Film* project has the same cast as Walter Asmus's 1991 production at the Gate Theatre, Dublin. There are very fine performances by all the actors. At the time of writing this is the only commercially available film of the play. In addition, a worthwhile production, directed by John Tydeman, is available on CD from Naxos AudioBooks.

BIBLIOGRAPHY

The following is a list of all the texts quoted from or referred to in the previous chapters.

PRIMARY

Beckett, S. (1959), *Molloy, Malone Dies, The Unnamable*. London: Calder and Boyars.

— (1963), *Watt*. London: Calder and Boyars.

— (1964), *How It Is*. London: John Calder.

— (1965a), *'Proust' and 'Three Dialogues with Georges Duthuit'*. London: John Calder.

— (1965b), *Waiting for Godot: A Tragicomedy in Two Acts* (2nd edn). London: Faber and Faber.

— (1966), *En attendant Godot: Pièce en deux actes*, C. Duckworth (ed.). London: Harrap.

— (1974), *Mercier and Camier*. London: Calder and Boyars.

— (1983), *Disjecta: Miscellaneous Writings and a Dramatic Fragment*, R. Cohn (ed.). London: John Calder.

— (1986), *The Complete Dramatic Works*. London and Boston: Faber and Faber.

— (1995), *The Complete Short Prose, 1929–1989*, S. E. Gontarski (ed.). New York: Grove Press.

— (1996), *Eleutheria*, B. Wright (trans.). London: Faber and Faber.

— (2006), *En attendant Godot / Waiting for Godot: Tragicomedy in 2 Acts: A Bilingual Edition*. New York: Grove Press.

Gontarski, S. E. (ed.) (1992), *The Theatrical Notebooks of Samuel Beckett: Vol. II: 'Endgame', with a Revised Text*. London: Faber and Faber.

Harmon, M. (ed.) (1998), *No Author Better Served: The Correspondence of Samuel Beckett and Alan Schneider*. Cambridge, Mass. and London: Harvard University Press.

McMillan, D. and Knowlson, J. (eds) (1993), *The Theatrical Notebooks of Samuel Beckett: Vol.1: 'Waiting for Godot', with a Revised Text*. London: Faber and Faber.

SECONDARY

Ackerley, C. J. and Gontarski, S. E. (2004), *The Grove Companion to Samuel Beckett: A Reader's Guide to His Works, Life, and Thought*. New York: Grove Press.

Aslan, O. (1988), *Roger Blin and Twentieth-Century Playwrights*, R. Cohn (trans.). Cambridge: Cambridge University Press.

Atkins, A. (1987), 'The structure of Lucky's speech (1966)', in Cohn (ed.), pp. 95–6.

Bentley, E. (1987), 'An anti-play (1964)', in Cohn (ed), pp. 23–4.

Ben-Zvi, L. (1991), 'Teaching *Godot* from life', in Schlueter and Brater (eds), pp. 37–41.

Boxall, P. (ed.) (2000), *Samuel Beckett: 'Waiting for Godot' / 'Endgame': A Reader's Guide to Essential Criticism*. Cambridge: Icon.

— (2004), 'Beckett and homoeroticism', in L. Oppenheim (ed.), *Palgrave Advances in Samuel Beckett Studies*. Basingstoke and New York: Palgrave Macmillan, pp. 110–32.

Bradby, D. (2001), *Beckett: 'Waiting for Godot' (Plays in Production)*. Cambridge: Cambridge University Press.

Brater, E. (ed.) (1986), *Beckett at 80 / Beckett in Context*. Oxford: Oxford University Press.

Brewer, M. M. (1987), 'A semiosis of waiting (1985)', in Cohn (ed.), pp. 150–5.

Chaudhuri, U. (1991), 'Who is Godot? A semiotic approach to Beckett's play', in Schlueter and Brater (eds), pp. 133–40.

Cohn, R. (1980), *Just Play: Beckett's Theater*. Princeton, N. J.: Princeton University Press.

— (1986), 'Growing (up?) with *Godot*', in Brater (ed.), pp. 13–24.

— (2001), *A Beckett Canon*. Ann Arbor: University of Michigan Press.

— (ed.) (1987), *Samuel Beckett, 'Waiting for Godot': A Casebook*. London: Macmillan.

Connor, S. (1988), *Samuel Beckett: Repetition, Theory and Text*. Oxford and New York: Basil Blackwell.

— (1992), 'Over Samuel Beckett's dead body', in Wilmer (ed.), pp. 100–8.

Cousineau, T. (1990), *'Waiting for Godot': Form in Movement*. Boston: Twayne.

Croall, J. (2005), *The Coming of Godot: A Short History of a Masterpiece*. London: Oberon Books.

Dettmar, K. J. H. (1999), 'The Joyce that Beckett built', in Stewart (ed.), pp. 78–92.

Duckworth, C. (1972), *Angels of Darkness: Dramatic Effect in Samuel Beckett with Special Reference to Eugène Ionesco*. London: George Allen & Unwin.

— (1987), 'Beckett's new *Godot*', in J. Acheson and K. Arthur (eds), *Beckett's Later Fiction and Drama: Texts for Company*. New York: St Martin's Press, pp. 175–92.

Dutton, R. (1986), *Modern British Tragicomedy and the British Tradition*. Norman and London: University of Oklahoma Press.

Esslin, M. (1976), *'Godot*, the authorized version'. *Journal of Beckett Studies*, No. 1, 98–100.

Fletcher, B. S., Fletcher, J., Smith, B. and Bachem, W. (1978), *A Student's Guide to the Plays of Samuel Beckett*. London and Boston: Faber and Faber.

Fletcher, J. (2000), *Samuel Beckett: A Faber Critical Guide: 'Waiting for Godot'; 'Endgame'; 'Krapp's Last Tape'*. London: Faber and Faber.

Garner, S. B. Jr (1991), 'Teaching the theatre, teaching *Godot*', in Schlueter and Brater (eds), pp. 141–8.

Gidal, P. (1987), 'Dialogue and dialectic in *Godot*', in Cohn (ed.), pp. 155–8.

Goldman, M. (1986), 'Vitality and deadness in Beckett's plays', in Brater (ed.), pp. 67–83.

Gontarski, S. E. (1985), *The Intent of 'Undoing' in Samuel Beckett's Dramatic Texts*. Bloomington: Indiana University Press.

Goodall, J. R. (2006), 'Lucky's energy', in S. E. Gontarski and A. Uhlmann (eds), *Beckett after Beckett*. Gainesville: University Press of Florida, pp. 187–96.

Gordon, L. (2002), *Reading 'Godot'*. New Haven and London: Yale University Press.

Graver, L. (2004), *Samuel Beckett: 'Waiting for Godot'* (2nd edn). Cambridge: Cambridge University Press.

Graver, L. and Federman, R. (eds) (1979), *Samuel Beckett: The Critical Heritage*. London: Routledge and Kegan Paul.

Haynes, J. and Knowlson, J. (2003), *Images of Beckett*. Cambridge: Cambridge University Press.

Hutchings, W. (1991), '*Waiting for Godot* and the principle of uncertainty', in Schlueter and Brater (eds), pp. 26–30.

— (2005), *Samuel Beckett's 'Waiting for Godot': A Reference Guide*. London and Westport, CT: Praeger.

Iser, W. (1992), 'Counter-sensical comedy and audience response in Beckett's *Waiting for Godot*', in S. Connor (ed.), *'Waiting for Godot' and 'Endgame': Contemporary Critical Essays*. London: Macmillan, pp. 55–70.

Janvier, L. (1969), *Samuel Beckett par lui-même*. Paris: Minuit.

Johnson, S. (1984), *Samuel Johnson: A Critical Edition of the Major Works*, D. Greene (ed.). Oxford and New York: Oxford University Press.

Kalb, J. (1989), *Beckett in Performance*. Cambridge: Cambridge University Press.

Keats, J. (1947), *The Letters of John Keats* (3rd edn), M. B. Forman (ed.). London, New York, Toronto: Oxford University Press.

Kenner, H. (1973), *A Reader's Guide to Samuel Beckett*. London: Thames & Hudson.

Knowlson, J. (1992), 'Beckett as director', in S. E. Wilmer (ed.), pp. 9–24.

— (1996), *Damned to Fame: The Life of Samuel Beckett*. London: Bloomsbury.

— (1999), 'My texts are in a terrible mess', in Stewart (ed.), pp. 176–86.

— and Knowlson, E. (eds) (2006), *Beckett Remembering, Remembering Beckett: Uncollected Interviews with Samuel Beckett and Memories of Those Who Knew Him*. London: Bloomsbury.

Kojève, A. (1969), *Introduction to the Reading of Hegel: Lectures on the 'Phenomenology of Spirit'* [1947], J. H. Nichols Jr (trans.), A. Bloom (ed.). Ithaca and London: Cornell University Press.

Lyons, C. R. (1983) *Samuel Beckett*. London and Basingstoke: MacMillan.

Mays, J. (1987), 'Allusion and echo in *Godot*', in Cohn (ed.), pp. 158–67.

McMillan, D. and Fehsenfeld, M. (1988), *Beckett in the Theatre: The Author as Practical Playwright and Director: Vol 1: From 'Waiting for Godot' to 'Krapp's Last Tape'*. London: John Calder.

Moorjani, A. (1998), '*En attendant Godot* on Michel Polac's *Entrée des Auteurs*', in M. Buning, D. De Ruyter, M. Engelberts and S. Houppermans (eds), *Beckett Versus Beckett*. Amsterdam and Atlanta, GA.: Rodopi, pp. 47–56.

— (2003), 'Diogenes lampoons Alexandre Kojève: cultural ghosts in Beckett's early French plays', in L. Ben-Zvi (ed.), *Drawing on Beckett: Portraits, Performances, and Cultural Contexts*. Tel Aviv: Assaph, pp. 69–88.

Oppenheim, L. (1994), *Directing Beckett*. Ann Arbor: University of Michigan Press.

Pilling, J. (2006), *A Samuel Beckett Chronology*. Basingstoke and New York: Palgrave Macmillan.

Pound, E. (1960), *The Literary Essays of Ezra Pound*, T. S. Eliot (ed.). London: Faber and Faber.

Priestley, J. B. (1975), *Particular Pleasures: Being a Personal Record of Some Varied Arts and Many Different Artists*. London: Heinemann.

Robbe-Grillet, A. (1965), 'Samuel Beckett, or "presence" in the theatre', in M. Esslin (ed.), *Samuel Beckett: A Collection of Critical Essays*. Englewood Cliffs, N. J.: Prentice-Hall, pp. 108–16.

Ross, C. (2001), 'Beckett's *Godot* in Berlin: new coordinates of the void', in A. Moorjani and C. Veit (eds), *Samuel Beckett:*

BIBLIOGRAPHY

Endlessness in the Year 2000 / Samuel Beckett: Fin sans Fin dans L'an 2000. Amsterdam and New York: Rodopi, pp. 64–73.

Scherzer, D. (1991), 'Teaching *Waiting for Godot* in a French drama course', in Schlueter and Brater (eds), pp. 90–8.

Schlueter, J. and Brater, E. (eds) (1991), *Approaches to Teaching Beckett's 'Waiting for Godot'*. New York: Modern Language Association of America.

Simon, R. K. (1987), 'Beckett, comedy and the critics', in Cohn (ed.), pp. 111–13.

Simpson, M. S. (1991), '*Waiting for Godot* and the forms of tragedy', in Schlueter and Brater (eds), pp. 79–84.

States, B. O. (1978), *The Shape of Paradox: An Essay on 'Waiting for Godot'*. Berkeley, Los Angeles and London: University of California Press.

Stewart, B. (ed.) (1999), *Beckett and Beyond*. Gerrards Cross, Bucks.: Colin Smythe.

Wilmer, S. E. (ed.) (1992), *Beckett in Dublin*. Dublin: Lilliput Press.

Wordsworth, W. (1988), *Selected Prose*, J. O. Hayden (ed.). Harmondsworth: Penguin.

Yeats, W. B. (1968), *Essays and Introductions*. New York: Collier.

Zeifman, H. (1987), 'The alterable whey of words: the play's texts (1977)', in Cohn (ed.), pp. 86–95.

Zinman, T. S. (1991), 'Teaching *Godot* through set and poster design', in Schlueter and Brater (eds), pp. 149–55.

122

INDEX